Genealogy in Ontario:
Searching the Records

Brenda Dougall Merriman

BA, CGRS, CGL

Maps: William J. Fraser

Inner Cover Maps: Fred Hill

Cover: Laurie Mackinnon
Christine Merriman

Ontario Genealogical Society

Canadian Cataloguing in Publication Data

Merriman, Brenda Dougall
  Genealogy in Ontario: searching the records

Rev.
Bibliography: p.
ISBN 1-55034-311-4

1. - Ontario - Genealogy - Handbooks, Manuals, etc.
I. - Ontario Genealogical Society. II. Title

CS88.058M47 1988 929'.1'.0720713 C88-0938097-2

ISBN 1-55034-311-4

Printed in Canada

PREFACE to the FIRST EDITION

The popularity of genealogy and family history research has increased tremendously in Ontario as elsewhere in the last few years, particularly stimulated by our Canadian Centennial year in 1967, and by the Ontario Bicentennial in 1984. The number of genealogical requests now being received by public and private institutions has risen dramatically.

Despite this growth in interest, only brief guides to genealogical sources for tracing Ontario families have yet been available, and no comprehensive handbook has been published. The vast size of our province and its many excellent record groups have made it difficult to produce more than regional or local guides. This publication is designed to help meet that deficiency by providing an overview of basic resources.

Each ancestor hunter begins with different information, a different starting point, or eventually meets different problems. Therefore this book does not give you a step-by-step lesson, nor might it answer every question that could arise in your research. Throughout the text we will refer to books, articles, and manuals which we feel are essential to good research (see full listings in Appendix II). We recommend that this book *Genealogy in Ontario: Searching the Records* be used in conjunction with another OGS publication, *Some Ontario References and Sources for the Family Historian,* as the latter contains an excellent bibliographic guide.

This particular book will deal with sources in our two largest repositories, the Public Archives of Canada (PAC) and the Archives of Ontario (AO). We hope to show where the records are, information needed to use them, their genealogical value, and some limitations or drawbacks associated with finding and using them.

Readers who pursue their searches in archives, museums, and libraries are advised to allow enough time to become familiar with each system and to learn locations of material sought.

BDM
1984

PREFACE to the SECOND EDITION

The experience of writing the first edition of this book has brought home the need to emphasize the two largest resource centres of Ontario material for genealogical research -- the National Archives of Canada (PAC) in Ottawa, and the Archives of Ontario (AO) in Toronto. The National Archives was formerly known as the Public Archives of Canada, and the long-used PAC designation will continue in this publication. Both centres contain so many records in one location that the researcher can save precious time. Visits to several locations such as municipal offices, churches, cemeteries, libraries, museums, courthouses and land registry offices may be avoided or shortened by using the microfilm copies of records deposited at PAC or AO.

This method of procedure in your family research leaves you more time on a local visit to pursue records and sources that are unique to the area, sources that have not been microfilmed, transcribed, published or indexed. This benefits those researchers who have easier access to Ottawa or Toronto than to a smaller community, or who do not live in the area of their research. Sometimes we who live in Ontario forget that there are many thousands of non-residents with ancestral roots here in the province. It should be realized, though, that certain PAC and AO sources are available in or through smaller local repositories.

The Ontario Genealogical Society's (OGS) publication *Some Ontario References and Sources for the Family Historian*, which was suggested as a companion volume to this book, is not being reprinted. We hope that this improved and revised *Genealogy in Ontario*: *Searching the Records* with its additional material will serve as a more complete reference for genealogical sources in the province, although each new discovery of source material and each new issue of a genealogical periodical can change the methods and results of family history. Readers who find errors or omissions herein are welcome to submit notes to OGS.

OGS owes a great debt to the work pioneered by the late Marion C. Keffer, Audrey L. Kirk UE and Robert F. Kirk, and to their successors Barbara B. Aitken, Dawn Broughton and the late Yvonne Crouch UE.

Genealogists have been spurned by professional records keepers and scorned by academics because of a perceived or sometimes real lack of professionalism in their methods or preparation. One does not have to engage in research for money to employ accepted standards in documenting a pedigree or family history. Hard work on the part of leading genealogists and their organizations continues to promote and elevate research standards and to educate novice researchers. There is an onus on all of us to address these problems. The way in which we go about our research, in public or private sources, and the tangible result of our work, can be a testament to the recognition of genealogy as a serious and important contribution to related social studies.

Let's remember to prepare diligently, ask intelligent questions, cite and acknowledge all sources, and do unto others. Let's expand in all ways and become family historians, not merely genealogists.

BDM
1988

ACKNOWLEDGMENTS

The author takes responsibility for any errors or omissions that may have crept into the text due to video display terminal fatigue and the demands of optical scan printing. However, the production of this book owes much to the ongoing support of many friends, and to the encouraging and constructive reviews offered by colleagues across the continent. My special thanks to the following:

--The many Ontario Genealogical Society members who gave advice and personal encouragement over the past few years, especially Claudia McArthur, Ruth Holt, Bill Zuefelt, Norman Crowder, Ryan Taylor, Judith A. Mitton and Brian Gilchrist. I was remiss in not thanking previous proofreaders Barbara Aitken and Helen Thompson.

--Thomas Hillman, Patricia Kennedy and Bennett Mc-Cardle at the National Archives of Canada.

--June Gibson, John Mezaks, Richard Ramsey, Catherine Shepard and Leon Warmski at the Archives of Ontario.

--Bill Fraser who came to the rescue with a fine set of maps, and Fred Hill who supplied the original inner cover maps.

--My husband, who humours and subsidizes the genealogy virus despite occasional unendurable seizures.

Both editions of this book benefitted from the patient guidance and expert assistance of Jim Kennedy.

TABLE OF CONTENTS

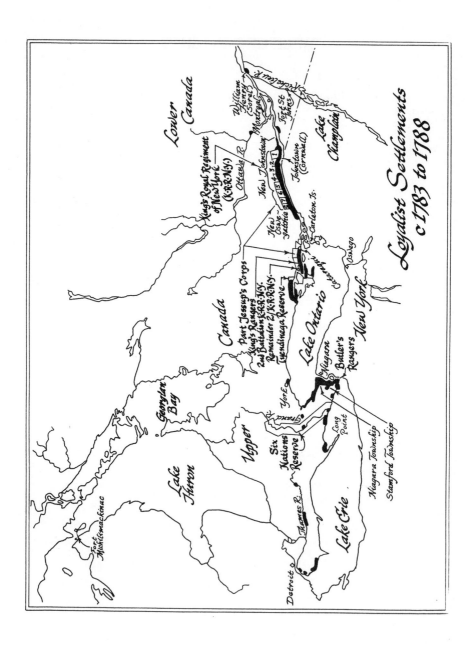

Loyalist Settlements c.1783 to 1788

Lower Canada

William Henry (Sorel)
Montreal
Fort St. Johns
Ottawa R.
Richelieu R.
Lake Champlain

King's Royal Regiment of New York (KRRNY)

New Johnstown
Johnstown (Cornwall)

Districts 1, 2, 3, 4, 5, 6, 7, 8

New Oswegatchie
Carleton Is.

Part Jessup's Corps
King's Rangers
2nd Battalion KRRNY.
Remainder 2/KRRNY.
(Tyendinaga Reserve)

Canada

Upper

Georgian Bay

Lake Huron

Lake Ontario

Osnabruck

Osnego

Fort Michilimackinac

New York

Niagara
Butler's Rangers

York

Six Nations Reserve

Grand

Long Point

Lake Erie

Detroit

Thames R.

Niagara Township
Stamford Township

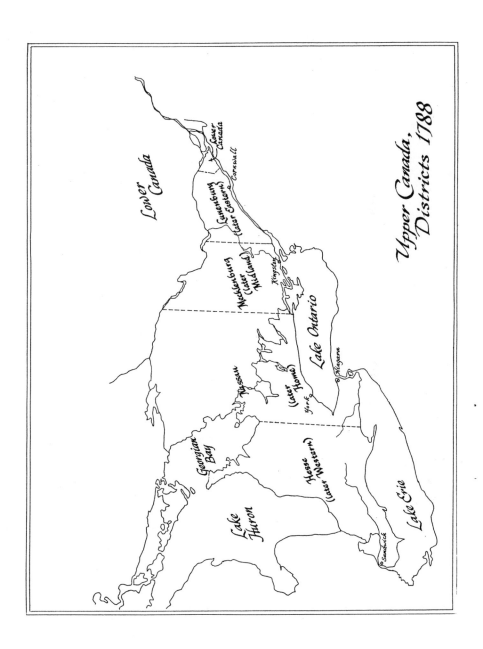

Upper Canada,
Districts 1788

Lower Canada

Lower
Canada

Cornwall

Luneburg
(later Eastern)

Mecklenburg
(later Midland)

Kingston

Lake Ontario

Nassau
(later Home)

York

Niagara

Georgian
Bay

Hesse
(later Western)

Lake
Huron

Sandwich

Lake Erie

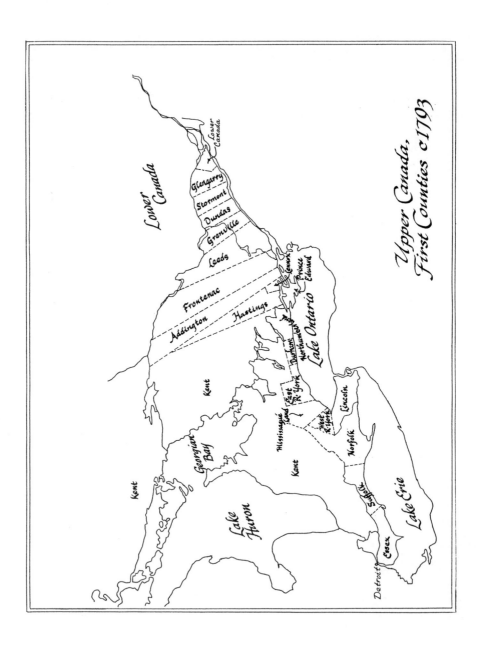

Upper Canada,
First Counties c1793

Lower Canada

Lower Canada

Glengarry
Stormont
Dundas
Grenville
Leeds
Frontenac
Addington
Hastings
Lennox
Prince Edward
Lake Ontario
Northumberland
Durham
East R. York
West R. York
Lincoln
Norfolk
Suffolk
Essex
Detroit
Lake Erie
Mississauga Land
Kent
Kent
Kent
Georgian Bay
Lake Huron

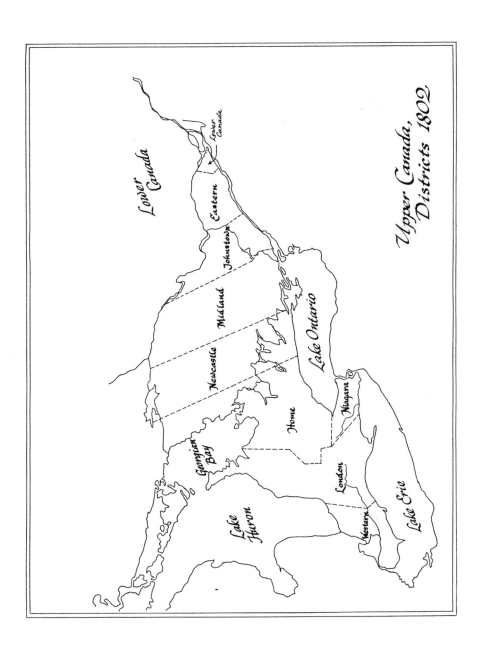

Upper Canada, Districts 1802

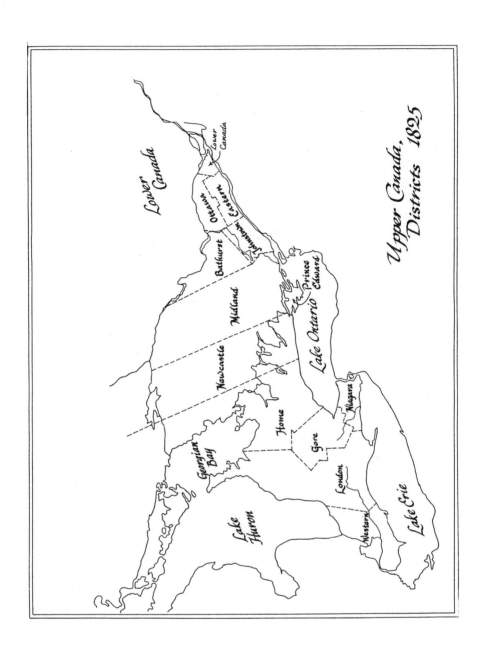

Upper Canada, Districts 1825

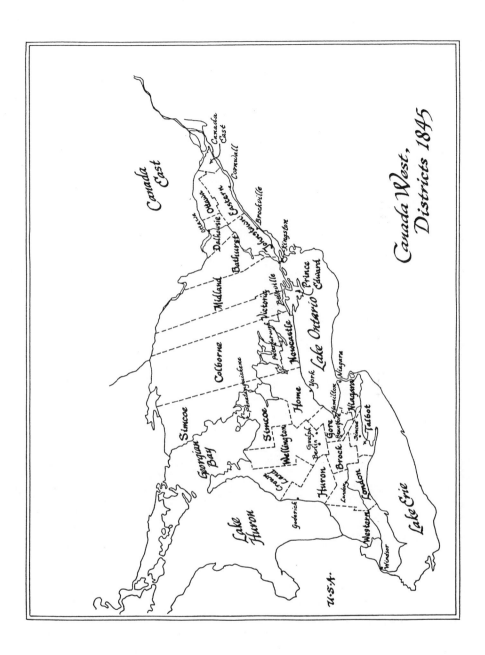

Canada West, Districts 1845

COUNTIES AND DISTRICTS OF ONTARIO

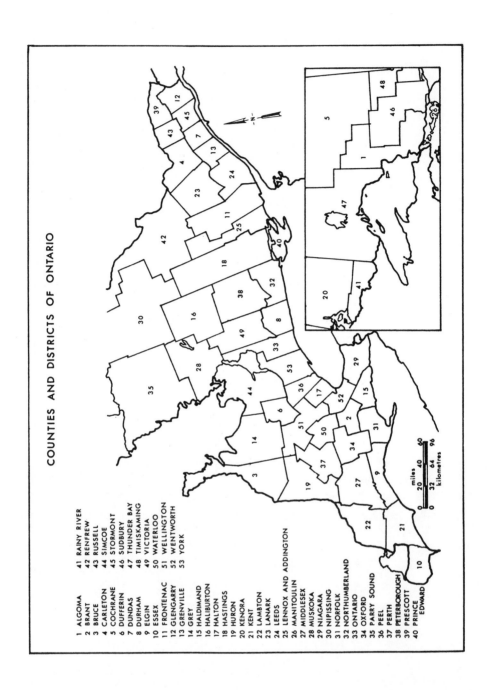

1 ALGOMA	41 RAINY RIVER
2 BRANT	42 RENFREW
3 BRUCE	43 RUSSELL
4 CARLETON	44 SIMCOE
5 COCHRANE	45 STORMONT
6 DUFFERIN	46 SUDBURY
7 DUNDAS	47 THUNDER BAY
8 DURHAM	48 TIMISKAMING
9 ELGIN	49 VICTORIA
10 ESSEX	50 WATERLOO
11 FRONTENAC	51 WELLINGTON
12 GLENGARRY	52 WENTWORTH
13 GRENVILLE	53 YORK
14 GREY	
15 HALDIMAND	
16 HALIBURTON	
17 HALTON	
18 HASTINGS	
19 HURON	
20 KENORA	
21 KENT	
22 LAMBTON	
23 LANARK	
24 LEEDS	
25 LENNOX AND ADDINGTON	
26 MANITOULIN	
27 MIDDLESEX	
28 MUSKOKA	
29 NIAGARA	
30 NIPISSING	
31 NORFOLK	
32 NORTHUMBERLAND	
33 ONTARIO	
34 OXFORD	
35 PARRY SOUND	
36 PEEL	
37 PERTH	
38 PETERBOROUGH	
39 PRESCOTT	
40 PRINCE EDWARD	

Introduction

1763	Treaty of Paris; New France (including present day Ontario) became a colony of Great Britain
1775-1783	American Revolutionary War
1783	Treaty of Separation; final influx of Loyalist refugees and British soldiers into Nova Scotia and Quebec
1783-1784	Spread of Loyalists and soldiers into western Quebec (now Ontario) under Governor Haldimand's supervision
1788	Western Quebec divided into four administrative districts
1789	Lord Dorchester created UE (Unity of Empire) designation and privileges for Loyalist settlers
1791	Constitutional Act; Quebec divided into Upper and Lower Canada
1792	Legislative Assembly of Upper Canada met at the capital, Newark (now Niagara-on-the-Lake)
1793	York (now Toronto) became the permanent capital of Upper Canada
1812-1814	War between Canada and the United States
1829	Welland Canal opened
1832	Rideau Canal opened
1834	First railway, at London
1837	Rebellion in Upper Canada, Reformers vs Establishment
1841	Act of Union; Upper and Lower Canada became Canada West and Canada East
1849	Districts abolished in favour of county administration
1850	Municipal Act; local government (towns and townships) became responsible for municipal business
1866	Fenian raids into Canada from the U.S.
1867	British North America Act; Canadian Confederation of four provinces; Canada West became Ontario
1885	Canadian Pacific Railway completed across Canada

Hints for the Beginning Genealogist

GROUP
CONTACT

For personal contact and do-it-yourself approaches, you should investigate joining a local genealogical society and genealogical research courses. Such courses might be conducted as evening classes or one-day weekend seminars by groups like genealogical or historical societies, libraries, archives, museums or com-

1

munity colleges. They may also take the form of "continuing education" programmes at high schools and universities.

REFERENCE BOOKS

The beginner's first step, collecting family information from sources at home and relatives, is well-described in dozens of reference books which should be available at a nearby library, wherever you live. One example is *Searching For Your Ancestors* by Gilbert Doane. (See full listings in Appendix II).

Procedures and methods for research may also be found in many books. The author recommends *Genealogical Research Methods and Sources, Vol. 1* edited by Milton Rubincam, or Stevenson's *Search and Research*. Books more specific to Canada and Ontario are *The Canadian Genealogical Handbook, In Search of Your Roots, Readings in Ontario Genealogical Sources*, and *Some Ontario References and Sources for the Family Historian*. As some of these are out of print, check with your local library for access to copies of these books.

Although this book will not go into research methods, there are a few notes included at the end of this chapter on organizing the material you collect. Certain words and terms occur frequently in the genealogical process and must be understood by the beginner. Doing actual research in Ontario also invites some pre-knowledge of resource centres and their systems, which will follow after this general introduction to the province.

SETTLEMENT OF ONTARIO

Settlement in Ontario by non-native peoples was initiated in an organized political way in 1783, although French fur traders, missionaries and scattered settlers had established earlier small communities. The arrival of the Loyalists and disbanded King's soldiers forced the British to open "new" territory in the late eighteenth and early nineteenth centuries.

In 1639 a noted settlement began that existed for a ten year period at Ste.-Marie among the Hurons, now re-created at Midland, Ontario. At the height of its existence the community numbered up to 66 people of French background. The names of 47 laymen of this time are printed in "The Earliest Ontarioans" in the OGS *Bulletin*, Vol. 9, No. 3 (1970). Thousands of their descendants live in Canada today and with some proof of lineage they can be officially recognized with a scroll created by a government committee. The scroll mentions any details of the ancestor as learned from existing records.

2

One suggestion for background reading of this period is *Upper Canada: The Formative Years* by Gerald Craig. Depending on the time period and the specific location of your ancestors, you may find more interest in a local history (see Aitken's *Bibliography* and Appendix II).

MAPS

One should always bear in mind that settlement grew along transportation routes, i.e. rivers and lakes, and later, roads, canals and railways. Thus it was along the Great Lakes water route and the rivers feeding it, that the population first grew, and from which it spread. With this in mind, a map will help in following movements of the second generation. A town on the settler's route to his final destination might have been the place for a stopover for many reasons, and could have been the location for a "missing" birth or marriage.

Try to obtain a map, preferably of pre-1968 vintage, i.e. before regional government led to changes in boundaries and placenames. The relatively new regional governments have grouped many smaller municipalities together for wide administrative purposes, sometimes but not always along former county boundaries. For genealogical research you can ignore these changes, unless you are trying to locate a previous township or county name on a current map.

Regional Name	Former County or Township Names
Metropolitan Toronto	southern part of York County: townships of York, Etobicoke, Scarborough..
York	northern part of York County: townships of Vaughan, Markham, King, Whitchurch, East & North Gwillimbury, Georgina.
Haldimand-Norfolk	Haldimand and Norfolk Counties.
Niagara	Lincoln and Welland Counties.
Hamilton-Wentworth	Wentworth County minus a northwest portion of Beverly township.
Waterloo	Waterloo County plus a northwest portion of Beverly township
Halton	Halton County.
Peel	Peel County.
Durham	Ontario County and some townships in Durham County: Cartwright, Darlington and Clarke.
Sudbury	Created from the former Sudbury District. Communities: Sudbury, Copper Cliff, Levack, Chelmsford,

3

Lively, Coniston, Falconbridge, Capreol, Nickel Centre, Onaping, Val Caron, Val Therese, Blezard Valley, Garson.

Ottawa-Carleton   Carleton County plus Cumberland township from Russell County.

Highly recommended is Perly's *Detail Atlas, Province of Ontario*, a series of maps showing not only regional governments but also fairly large scale maps of all counties and northern districts. All township names are indexed as well as all placenames and waterways. A map called "Geographic Townships in the Province of Ontario" is also available from the Ontario Ministry of Natural Resources (see Appendix I). See also Betty Kidd's article "Maps in Genealogical Research" in *Families*, Vol. 16, No. 4 (1977).

As the population grew, the original boundaries and jurisdictions of government changed from time to time to deal with increasingly specific administrative and legal needs. The changes affect the location of certain records. "The Districts and Counties of Ontario, 1777-1979, Two Centuries of Evolution" by Eric Jonasson (*Families*, Vol. 20, No. 2 (1981) is the standard and complete reference on this subject.

The **township**,divided into concessions and then into lots, was the basic unit for land surveys. The geographic boundaries of townships remained relatively unchanged in the province until some "disappeared"with the advent of regional government.

At the beginning of this chapter we have reproduced a series of maps to show some of the developments in the eighteenth and nineteenth centuries.

Discovering Residential Locations

After collecting all the information available from your family members, your next goal is to find your ancestral **location** in Ontario, if a specific reference has not yet turned up. Location -- county, town or township -- is of the utmost importance in order to access the appropriate records. What can you do if your only reference is to "Upper Canada", "British Canada", "English Canada" or "Canada West", all used to indicate early Ontario? For the sake of consistency, it will be called **Ontario** throughout the text.

4

INDEXES

The following are some indexes that might help with this most basic problem, indexes that apply to the province as a whole:

Unpublished

Ontario (Computerized) Land Records Index
Index to Upper Canada Land Petitions
Index to Surrogate Clerk's Applications Books
(all described in later chapters)

Published

OGS, *Index to the 1871 Census of Ontario* (ongoing publication of county or regional areas)
Reid, *The Loyalists in Ontario*
Reid, *Marriage Notices of Ontario*
Wilson, *Ontario Marriage Notices*
Wilson, *Marriage Bonds of Ontario 1803-1834*
McKenzie, *Death Notices from the Christian Guardian, 1836-1850*
McKenzie, *Death Notices from the Christian Guardian, 1851-1860*
McKenzie, *More Notices from Methodist Newspapers, 1830-1857*
The Ontario Register 7 vols.
People of Ontario, 1600-1900 3 vols.
Whyte, *A Dictionary of Scottish Emigrants to Canada Before Confederation*
Wilson, *Directory of the Province of Ontario, 1857.*

The second group of sources above is obviously not primary material with the exception of the 1871 census index, as a reference to a primary record. All indexes by their human transcription are subject to error. All should be used with caution; the books will not be comprehensive or inclusive of every person in the province. For example, *People of Ontario, 1600-1900* deals largely with late nineteenth century historical atlases and local histories. The indexes do provide clues to locations of the surname, and sometimes even the exact individual sought. In *Directory of the Province of Ontario* the representation is mainly among business and prominent people of the communities. It goes almost without saying that the degree of difficulty in this kind of search for names is directly proportional to the commonness of the surname.

SPELLING

When searching old handwritten indexes to any set of records, or almost any index for that matter, great care must be taken to examine all variations of spelling that your surname might have engendered. The majority of our ancestors at the birth of this province and in later waves of immigration were not literate. Appearance of their names in written records was the work of a minister, local official, census enumerator, etc., who was free to spell his own interpretation. It helps to sound out the surname phonetically and imagine several variations, even on the seemingly simple name, for vowel and consonant changes.

AMBIGUOUS
PLACENAMES

There are many Ontario places with the same name in widely scattered areas, another good reason to have a map at hand. It is possible to start off on the wrong track entirely unless you are aware of this. If your ancestor's death certificate or obituary says he was born in York, does it mean the town of York (now Toronto), or the county of York, a considerably larger area with nine townships at one time? Does it mean the township of York in York County, or was it the village of York in Seneca Township, Haldimand County?

Here are a few examples of hundreds of multiple placename occurrences:

Perth	-	county in south central Ontario
	-	county town of Lanark County
Prescott	-	county along the Ottawa River
	-	town in Augusta Township, Grenville County
Clinton	-	township in Lincoln County
	-	village in Goderich Township, Huron County
Hamilton	-	city in Wentworth County
	-	township in Northumberland County
Simcoe	-	county west of Lake Simcoe
	-	county town of Norfold County.

Some original townships (a few examples are Dumfries, Zorra, Oxford, Tilbury and Sandwich) were later subdivided into East, West, North or South. Camden Township is in Kent County; Camden East Township is in Lennox & Addington County. Huron Township is not in Huron County; Brant Township is not in Brant County; Haldimand Township is not in Haldimand County. Oxford Township is in Grenville County, but Oxford East, West and North Townships are in Oxford County!

1871-1881
"SPECIAL"
ENUMERATION
DISTRICTS

Three "counties" that will not appear on these maps are the names **Bothwell**, **Cardwell**, and **Monck**. These were enumeration districts artificially created for the 1871 and later census returns. It can be confusing for the novice, particularly since the names Cardwell and Monck are also townships in Muskoka District, and

Bothwell refers as well to a village of the same name. See Chapter 4 for more details.

IDENTIFYING
NUMBERED
TOWNSHIPS

When the province was first being surveyed, some early townships were hastily numbered to accommodate the large numbers of arriving Loyalists and soldiers who needed land. As a result, some early land records may have such references as "the third township from the lake", or "the Quaker township". Referring to the first map of our series, townships along the north shore of the **St. Lawrence River** were:

1 - Charlottenburg	5 - Matilda
2 - Cornwall	6 - Edwardsburgh
3 - Osnabruck	7 - Augusta
4 - Williamsburgh	8 - Elizabethtown

Numbered townships in the **Bay of Quinte** area were:

1 - Kingston	4 - Adolphustown
2 - Ernestown	5 - Marysburgh
3 - Fredricksburg	

Then were added:

6 - Sophiasburg	9 - Thurlow
7 - Ameliasburg	10 - Richmond
8 - Sydney	11 - Camden

Early townships in the **Niagara** area:

1 - Niagara	2 - Stamford (first known as "Mountain" or "Mount Dorchester")

Land grants were also made early on in areas known as "Grand River" and "Thames River" (see map 1) before township surveys were made. The Thames River was known as La Tranche for some years. Numbered townships along the **Thames River** were:

(South side)	(North Side)
1 - Raleigh	1 - Dover
2 - Harwich	2 - Chatham
3 - Howard	3 - Camden

The original Crown grant of six miles on either side of the Grand River to the Six Nations Indians came to include eight townships in Haldimand County, four in Brant County, three in Waterloo County and two in Wellington County.

In *Families*, Vol. 15, No. 4 (1976), Eldon Weber writes on "Some Unusual Aspects of Early Land Surveys in

Old Ontario". This article explores the effect that some very large land grants had on early survey patterns.

Some useful publications are Carter's two-volume *Place Names of Ontario* or the three volume *Places in Ontario, Their Names, Origins, and History* by Mika. A recent publication is *Guide to Southern Ontario Place Names for Family Researchers* by Mary K. Trace (see Appendix II).

Confusing place references in old records for some larger or more historical centres that had name changes might be sorted out by the following list:

Present Name Former Name

Present Name	Former Name
Burlington	Wellington Square
Cambridge	Galt, Hespeler, Preston
Cornwall	New Johnstown
Dundas	Coote's Paradise
Grimsby	Forty Mile Creek (The Forty)
Halton Hills	Acton, Georgetown
Hespeler	New Hope
Jordan	Twenty Mile Creek (The Twenty)
Kingston	Cataraqui
Kitchener	Berlin
Mississauga	Toronto township
Nanticoke	Townsend, Woodhouse, Walpole townships
Niagara Falls	Clifton, Drummondville, Chippawa
Niagara-on-the-Lake	Newark
Orillia	The Narrows
Oshawa	Kerr's Creek
Ottawa	Bytown
Paris	Forks of the Grand
St. Catharines	Twelve Mile Creek (The Twelve)
St. Thomas	Stirling
Thunder Bay	Port Arthur (Prince Arthur's Landing), Fort William
Toronto	York
Wallaceburg	Baldoon
Whitby	Windsor, Perry's Corners
Windsor	Sandwich
Woodstock	Town Plot

Official agencies that will attempt to answer your questions about "lost" names are:

Nomenclature Section
Ontario Geographic Names Board
Whitney Block, Room 2601
99 Wellesley Street West
Toronto, Ontario
M7A 1W3.

Secretariat, Geographical Names
615 Booth Street
Ottawa, Ontario
K1A 0E9

LOCATING PROPERTY DESCRIPTION

Once you have located your family, you will eventually need to pin down their exact location or legal description of property they held in a town or township. Land records are accessible this way and so often they are the only source for genealogical information in the province's earliest days. Sources for the property description might be the Ontario Land Records Index if a Crown land grant was involved, an Agricultural Schedule of a census return, local atlases and histories, or documents found from the county, township or town deeds indexes.

Most historical atlases for Ontario counties also show township maps with landowners' names. Be aware that names are usually owners **at the time of publication**, and not necessarily original owners or Crown grants. Published mainly in the last half of the nineteenth century, these atlases for southern Ontario counties and more northerly districts have been reprinted within the last few years (see Appendix II).

Where a town or city is the location, a directory with street addresses may be the best source. An address can then lead to the legal property description on land registry plans. Assessment rolls, if available, will serve the same purpose.

FINDING EMIGRANTS' ORIGINS

The ultimate goal in the Ontario ancestor hunt is to learn the previous residence of the immigrant to Ontario so that research can continue in another province, state or country. A minor note here is that not all immigrants came here from overseas. Many arrived from the United States and from other Canadian provinces, so strictly speaking we use the terms "previous residence" or "overseas/overland origin". Ontario records, like those of any other "new world" country, have limitations in this respect. Such records as census returns, death certificates or marriage certificates will likely state birthplace as merely, for instance, "U.S." or "Scotland". You are going to need the name of a town, village, parish, or at least a county type of jurisdiction to be able to research elsewhere successfully.

Sources that should be investigated for this important clue are cemetery inscriptions, obituaries, land petitions, military lists, Loyalist claims, ships' lists, marriage records, local histories and directories. Historical atlases sometimes have biographies of prominent settlers or lists of inhabitants with birthplace and date of settlement. Chances are you may never discover exactly what you want, but perseverance is the only course. As an encouraging example, searches of all these records had failed to indicate where in Ireland one original emigrant had lived, other than "County Tyrone" in his land petition. Ironically, and by chance, we learned that the local school in his area had been named for his home parish in Ireland.

Canada Company Remittance Books at AO 1843-52 can provide connections between settlers in Ontario and their relatives overseas (see Chapter 5, Section A).

See my article "Documenting Your Emigrant Ancestor" in *OGS Seminar Annual* (1987) for further illustration of this particular problem.

Organizing and Filing Your Records

In organizing the material you collect, try to keep impeccable notes. From the outset it is important to record not only all the details of a document, but also to record its exact source. Systematic organization is thoroughly described in excellent publications like Wright and Pratt's *Genealogical Research Essentials*, or Jonasson's *Untangling the Tree: Organizational Systems for the Family Historian*. The latter is very detailed and discusses one type of numbering system which can be applied to either manual or computer use.

A research **calendar** is a good way to keep track of the record you saw, its contents, exactly where you found it, and the date you searched it.

A good test of your system is to see if someone else can look at your files and understand the steps you have accomplished and where you are going next.

You should get used to evaluating the evidence that you find. In other words, consider your source. What your great-uncle Ned told you and what the officiating minister at the wedding wrote are not the same kind of sources. Keep an open, enquiring mind and train your mind to analyze your progress.

PRIMARY
SOURCES

Records made **at the time of the event**, by someone involved in the event, or a witness to it, are considered primary sources or evidence. Usually this includes birth certificates, baptismal records, marriage records, death certificates, wills, and any evidence sworn in court or before a magistrate. Even these sources can be suspect, as well as many other records that genealogists use, when they are dissected into several pieces of information from the one record. In the next chapters we will look at these sources more critically.

SECONDARY
SOURCES

Secondary sources, sometimes referred to as "circumstantial" evidence, mean records that were made some time **after** an event occurred, or that come from an indirect, uninvolved party. This can include "hearsay" or family traditions,undocumented family histories and other published material, and any information on a record or document given by a non-witness.

As an example of breaking down one record source into several pieces of information, a death date on a gravestone is presumed correct, since it was likely provided by the widowed spouse or a child who was nearby at death; a birth date or place on a gravestone is secondary evidence in the case of an older adult since it's unlikely that any heirs or family survivors were actually present at the birth or baptism of deceased. Newspaper notices and obituary information must be handled the same way. Typesetting errors were and still are a common occurrence in dates and spellings.

The genealogist tries to collect as much primary information as possible, but too often we find that records are missing, or unexplained gaps occur in the records that we have discovered. Then we rely on as much secondary material as is available. If you are aware of the limitations of the specific records and documents then you are more likely to keep that open mind while searching. We want to stress that every source should be regarded with a healthy objectivity until it can be reinforced with data from other sources. If we may quote Patricia Kennedy in *Families*, Vol. 16, No. 4 (1977), p. 198, "Do not blindly trust an isolated record."

PEDIGREE

As with any genealogical research, in Ontario you will want to trace back from the known to the unknown. The records you use and the steps you take will depend on your starting information and the time period. Working your way back in time from one generation to the previous one, painstaking and frustrating as it may be at times, is the only logical and acceptable way to plot your pedigree. By **pedigree** we mean your direct ancestors only, male and female, in each generation. This is a fundamental, or skeletal, chart.

You may only be interested in developing a straight-line or single line pedigree, a slightly different goal. This follows just one parent in each generation, of a single surname. Searching one family at a time is obviously less confusing and makes orderly note keeping easier.

Ideally, basic data on the pedigree for each ancestor will consist of his or her name with dates and places of birth, marriage, and death. In the absence of primary sources, circumstantial evidence should be gathered from all available secondary sources. In order to progress back each generation, proof of relationship, **identification**, is needed. In other words, this means proving the parents of each ancestor, through birth or baptismal records, marriage records, wills, etc.

GENEALOGY

Then there is the genealogical chart which traces all the descendants of one pair of ancestors. Brothers and sisters in each generation are included, along with their spouses and children. The written form of such a chart is a true **genealogy** that systematically records all known data on each person. A widely accepted format for constructing and numbering a genealogy is that used in the National Genealogy Society's (U.S.) *Quarterly* or as described in Doane's *Searching For Your Ancestors*.

GROUP SHEET

A common method of "storing" acquired information is the **family group sheet** whereby each male ancestor is shown on one page with his wife and children and all their relevant data. This is a convenient way to summarize or communicate family information.

More recently, computer software has been developed for the compilation, storage and communication of genealogical data, on prescribed forms as above. To date, *Computer Genealogy* by Anderek and Pence is the best guide to hardware and software. Many large genealogical organizations have computer sub-groups, and regularly publish user information.

FAMILY
HISTORY

A **family history** goes beyond the basic data by presenting more information about the individuals in each generation. The vital statistics are supplemented with additional information (geographical, historical, social, occupational, biographical) to make ancestors "come alive" in their contemporary context.

A family history has more appeal to a larger readership, not only to relatives but also to others interested in the same locality. If one of your goals is to publish, remember that most non-genealogists are turned off by a litany of names and dates, even though your scholarship may be admirable.

Whatever your goal as an end result of your research, please consider **donating a copy** of your publication, typed manuscript, or even your notes, to a genealogical society, archives, museum or library in the area where your family lived. These groups and institutions have made it possible for you to collect your information, and they have not always been treated well by eager genealogists. Help us build good relationships with our archivists and librarians by returning to them some of the fruits of your labours.

Researching in Resource Centres

REFERENCE
TERMS,
ABBREVIATIONS

The use of the term **finding aid** refers to readily available, on-site, archival reference aids that list or describe contents of a collection of records. **Inventories** and **calendars** are specific types of finding aids relevant to the structure of particular records collections. The abbreviations **RG** (record group) and **MG** (manuscript group) at PAC or **MU** and **MS** (manuscript collections) at AO are very common in cataloguing. Abbreviations used for main resource centres in the next chapters are listed in Appendix I with their addresses.

LOCAL
RESOURCE
CENTRES

All repositories that hold copies of records are not listed in this book. We suggest that as you proceed in your research you will become familiar with names of special and unique local collections. For names and addresses of Ontario local libraries, archives and museums, consult the handy *Canadian Almanac & Directory* published each year (full listing in Appendix II). Library addresses are listed as well in *Directory of Ontario Public Libraries*, a government publication through the Provincial Library Service. Filby's imminent new publication *Directory of Libraries with Local History/Genealogy Collections* will include data from more than sixty Ontario libraries.

Addresses of local historical societies in the province can be obtained from the Ontario Historical Society (Appendix I). The annual *Municipal Directory* published by the Ministry of Municipal Affairs gives addresses for municipal offices and local functions such as land registry offices, school boards, health units, etc. Ontario Government publications are available through government bookstores (Appendix II).

PAC & AO

Exact references to many records groups have not been included here, as a personal visit to PAC or AO neces-

13

sarily involves some orientation time. Also, the same records collection will likely have different reference numbers at each location. After registration at AO,the Archivist will give an overview of records and some instruction on the double cataloguing system. Most records sought at AO by genealogists are easily accessible in the main reading room with their two volume *Guide to Holdings.* At PAC you will be directed to the Division you need (Manuscripts, Government Archives, Maps,Library, etc). Finding aids for the most popularly used genealogical sources are concentrated in a reference room, with genealogical consultants available. Retrieval and microfilm readers are in a separate room. In both centres lockers are provided because you cannot bring briefcases and other personal belongings into the reading rooms. Identification is necessary to obtain a research pass, but there is no charge. It is wise to spend some time with the finding aid for a collection before jumping in with no terms of reference.

Most of the records groups are not "perfect" in their geographical coverage, their survival rate, nor in the amount of family information given. Generally speaking, the earlier the time period, the fewer records we have to work with. The challenge and satisfaction in genealogical research lie in finding and using all the accessible records to re-construct your ancestor's family.

GOVERNMENT RECORDS, POLICY

The majority of records used by genealogists were created by government, and this will continue in the future. Records affecting current research in Ontario might have previously been a federal or a provincial government jurisdiction. Existing policy for many ministries is to deposit older records, after a certain time lapse, in either the PAC or AO, such as census returns. However, **access** for us to those records is affected by the contemporary conditions under which a record was created, or by prevailing government policies on the right to privacy versus freedom of access.

Both the Canadian federal government (Access to Information Act) and the government of Ontario (Freedom of Information and Protection of Individual Privacy Act) have enacted freedom of information laws that now make accessible much **personal** material collected by them. In general, the material is contemporary and available only to the individual concerned, in order to safeguard against disclosure to unauthorized persons. No information is to be released about an individual without his consent.

14

As an example, the federal government now keeps more than 2,200 information databanks on its citizens. Its latest Act allows more access, in a genealogical context, to certain immigration and military records, after consulting the detailed *Access Register* or *Personal Information Index* and applying with the appropriate form. This is discussed in later relevant chapters of this book.

Similarly, the Ontario government has issued aids called *Directory of Personal Information Banks* and *Directory of General Records*. The types of records are described, their ministries and locations, and accessibility. Both sets of finding aids are available at public institutions such as libraries, post offices and government locations.

Policies of privacy versus access are reviewed often, and it is to be hoped that many such databanks will be available to our descendants for their genealogical pursuits, without being destroyed in the intervening years.

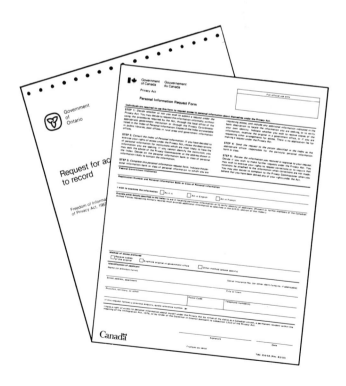

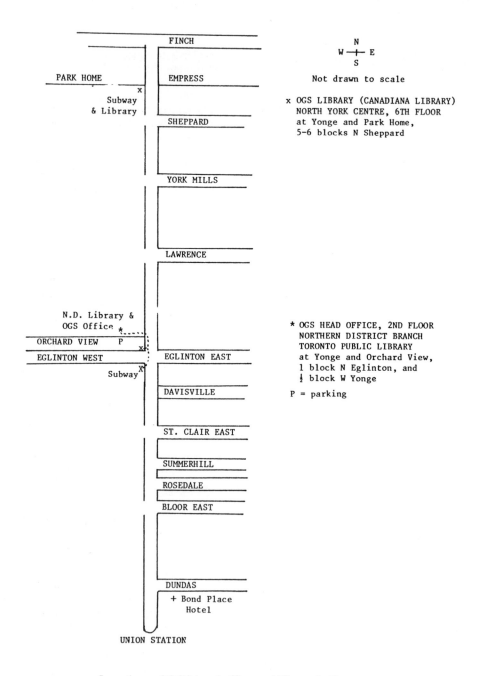

Locations of OGS head office and library in Toronto

1/ The Ontario Genealogical Society

The Ontario Genealogical Society (OGS) was founded in 1961 to serve the interests of genealogy and family history in this province. It has grown to become one of the largest such groups in North America. OGS Branches represent nearly every area of Ontario with their own newsletters, publications, meetings and projects. The 25th Anniversary celebrations in 1986 included the granting of a Coat of Arms to the Society by the Lord Lyon of Scotland. "Multi Priores Multi Patriae", the distinctive accompanying motto (which translates to "Many Ancestors, Many Homelands"), reflects the cultural background of our province.

At the main office in Toronto the Board of Management, Board of Directors and Committee meetings are held, and correspondence, memberships and distribution of publications are handled. In effect, this is our central core. The office staff do not do research, but will answer a query by sending general information. The emphasis in OGS has always been a "do-it-yourself" approach to genealogy.

STRUCTURE

Eleven Regional Directors and two Provincial Directors are elected to form the Board of Directors. From these, five officers are elected to the Board of Management. The Society has five Committee Divisions for Corporate Services, Educational Services, Publications, Regional Affairs, and Special Projects. Under these Divisions, more than thirty active committees are working on new or continuing OGS projects and goals. As well, OGS has liaison with or delegates to the Ontario Archives, the Canadian Federation of Genealogical & Family History Societies, the Federation of Family History Societies in Britain, and the Federation of Genealogical Societies based in the United States.

MEMBERSHIP

Membership benefits include the scholarly quarterly journal *Families*, the quarterly newsletter *Newsleaf*, the *Annual Report*, and a choice of purchasable publications. Full publications lists are featured in some issues of *Newsleaf* and the most popular and helpful books are listed in Appendix II. Members are allowed some free queries each year in "The Name Game", a regular *Families* section for contacting others of mutual ancestral interest. The basic membership fee also includes one membership in a branch of your choice. And of course every member is entitled to vote at and participate in the annual meeting, held in conjunction with the Seminar.

BRANCHES	Branch membership gives access to more localized source information and contacts. For instance, branches have their own meetings, workshops, newsletters, library collections, and cemetery transcriptions. Some have published guides to sources in their areas. Several branches form a Region, and day-long Regional Meetings are held once or twice a year. Branches are the "grassroots" of OGS and are your best value for local news and sources.

LIBRARY

The Society's library is housed in the Canadiana Collection of the North York Public Library, located in the North York Centre on Park Home Street west of Yonge Street in Metropolitan Toronto. **North York Centre** is the name of the subway stop for visitors. Microfilm readers can be booked in advance by telephone. The library staff cannot undertake research, but some OGS material is now available on Inter Library Loan (ILL). The exceptions to this policy are family histories, cemetery transcriptions, periodicals, fragile books, and historical atlases, maps and gazeteers. However, family histories and periodicals can be photocopied and most cemetery transcriptions are available for purchase from the branch that produced them.

OGS Library Holdings was intended as a handy reference for titles and call numbers, but since it was published in 1984, about 600 items were added through the Silver Anniversary Family History Collection. Microfilming of these sometime in the future will make them accessible through ILL.

OGS Library
Canadiana Collection, North York Library
North York Centre, 6th Floor
North York, Ontario
M2N 5N9   (416) 495-3427

Hours: Mon - Thurs 9 am - 8:30 pm
Fri - Sat 9 am - 5:30 pm

FAMILIES

In the following pages there will be many references to articles in *Families*, written by experts on sources that we all need to use for information. This quarterly, because of its continuity and the calibre of contributors, must be considered of prime value to anyone pursuing genealogy in Ontario. *Families* began in 1971 as Volume 10, the first nine volumes of the journal having been previously published as *The Bulletin*. If your nearest library with a genealogical collection, or your local genealogical society does not have *Families*, you might ask them to consider a purchase or exchange.

Back issues are available through the central office in Toronto.

SEMINAR

The highlight of the year is the annual seminar, which consists of three days of lectures, workshops and socializing. Each year a different branch is the host. While the focus of the seminar is on the host's area's resources, there is a also a variety of topics to appeal to all attendees. None of us should under-estimate this opportunity for personal contact with fellow members and expert speakers. The seminar is open to non-members as well. A *Seminar Annual*, a compendium of the weekend contributions and related material, has been published since 1983. Before this, seminar presentations were published in the fourth issue of *Families* each year.

PROJECTS

Special ongoing, long-range projects involving every branch of the Society are the transcriptions of over 5,000 cemeteries in Ontario.It is expected that the programme will be complete early in the 1990s. Cemetery transcriptions can be seen at the National Archives (PAC) in Ottawa, at the Archives of Ontario (AO) in Toronto, and at the OGS Library. The AO is very up to date in microfilming these acquisitions, but does not now participate in Inter Library Loan, although some plans are being made to change this. *Inventory of Cemeteries in Ontario*: *A Genealogical Research Guide* can be bought through the OGS office. It lists all known early cemeteries and their current status, i.e. accessibility in transcribed form. Most branches are selling, for a nominal sum, completed local transcriptions.

Indexing of the 1871 census (heads of families and "strays") has been completed and is being published at several volumes per year, each volume containing one or more counties. They are also available through the OGS office.

The OGS Church Records Inventory will catalogue nineteenth century churches in Ontario, arranged by religious denomination. Progress on these projects can be followed in *Newsleaf*, at branch or regional meetings, and in the Society's *Annual Report*.

HISTORY

Retrospects of the Society and the advancement of genealogy in Ontario have appeared in *Families*, Vol. 20, No. 4 (1981) by Kathleen M. Richards, "The Ontario Genealogical Society -- Twentieth Anniversary" and Vol. 26, No. 4 (1987) by Bruce Elliott, "Landmarks in Ontario Genealogy: A Twenty-Five Year Retrospective". As well, the *Report* of the twenty-fifth annual meeting (1986) contains early recollections.

OGS is grateful to the Ontario government's Ministry of Culture and Communications for its ongoing assistance and support.

MAIN
OFFICE

Ontario Genealogical Society
40 Orchard View Boulevard
Suite 253, 2nd Floor
Toronto, Ontario
M4R 1B9 (416) 489-0734
Hours: Mon - Fri 9 - 5

MULTI PATRIAE
PRIORES ❖ MULTAE

OGS Branches

Brant County   Box 2181, Brantford, Ont.
                    N3T 5Y6
Bruce & Grey   Box 1606, Port Elgin, Ont.
                    N0H 2C0

Elgin County	Box 416, St. Thomas, Ont. N5P 3V2
Essex County	Box 2 Station A, Windsor, Ont. N9A 6J5
Halton-Peel	Box 373, Oakville, Ont. L6J 5A8
Hamilton	Box 904, Hamilton, Ont. L8N 3P6
Huron County	Box 469, Goderich, Ont. N7A 5C7
Kawartha	Box 162, Peterborough, Ont. K9J 6Y8
Kent County	Box 964, Chatham, Ont. N7M 5L3
Kingston	Box 1394, Kingston, Ont. K7L 5C6
Lambton County	Box 2857, Sarnia, Ont. N7T 7W1
Leeds & Grenville	Box 536, Brockville, Ont. K6V 5V7
London	Box 871 Station B, London, Ont. N6A 4Z3
Niagara Peninsula	Box 2224 Station B, St. Catharines, Ont. L2M 6P6
Nipissing District	Box 93, North Bay, Ont. P1B 8G8
Norfolk County	Box 145, Delhi, Ont. N4B 2W9
Ottawa	Box 8346, Ottawa, Ont. K1G 3H8
Oxford County	Box 1092, Woodstock, Ont. N4S 8A5
Perth County	Box 9, Stratford, Ont. N5A 6S8
Quinte	Box 301, Bloomfield, Ont. K0K 1G0
Sault Ste. Marie & District	Box 1203, Sault Ste Marie, Ont. P6A 6N1
Simcoe County	Box 892, Barrie, Ont. L4M 4Y6
Sudbury District	c/o Sudbury Public Library, 200 Brady St., Sudbury, Ont. P3E 5K3
Thunder Bay District	Box 373 Station F, Thunder Bay, Ont. P7C 4V9
Toronto	Box 147 Station Z, Toronto, Ont. M5N 2Z3
Waterloo-Wellington	Box 603, Kitchener, Ont. N2G 4A2
Whitby-Oshawa	Box 174, Whitby, Ont. L1N 5S1

Macdonald Block
Parliament Buildings
Toronto, Ontario
M7A 1Y5

416/965-1687

416/965-6749

83-549993-5-01
--- BRENDA MERRIMAN
--- R.R. #1
--- PUSLINCH, ONTARIO

NOB 2J0

INFORMATION EXTRACTED FOR GENEALOGY

MARRIAGE

PLACE OF MARRIAGE: GLENGARRY

DATE OF MARRIAGE: JULY 15,1884

	GROOM	BRIDE
NAME:	MCMILLAN, HUGH	MCINTOSH, ANNIE
AGE:	27	25
PLACE OF BIRTH:	LOCHIEL	CHARLOTTENBURGH
RELIGION:	PRESBY.	PRESBY.
PARENTS NAMES		
FATHER:	MCMILLAN. ARCHIBALD	MCINTOSH. JOHN
MOTHER:	GRANT. MARGARET	MCDONALD. CATHERINE

WITNESSES: DUNCAN T. MCINTOSH
                     MARGARET ANN MCKAY

OFFICIATING CLERGY: ALEX MACPHERSON

REGISTRATION NUMBER: 1884-05-011169

ISSUED AT TORONTO
DECEMBER 2,1983

(MRS) K.V. BELL

MANAGER, CUSTOMER SERVICES

A "genealogical" marriage certificate from the Office of the Registrar General

2/ Post-1869 Vital Statistics

1869 Vital Statistics Act; civil registration required in Ontario

1892 Childrens' Aid Society opened first shelter, in Toronto

1921 First Adoption Act; Childrens' Aid Society assumed final responsibility

1930 Divorce Act; divorce became a provincial matter

CERTIFICATES

From 1 July 1869 births, marriages and deaths were **supposed** to be registered with the provincial government. This did not always happen, especially in the first years, for various reasons. Parties to an event were often negligent or ignorant of the law. Alternatives to official certificates for vital statistics are church records, cemetery records, funeral home records, attending physicians' statements, newspaper notices and obituaries, or whatever opportunity presents itself. One researcher obtained a midwife's statement to confirm his own birth. Hospitals are not known to be receptive or cooperative with genealogical requests, e.g. birth information; their files involving patients are considered private.

An application for a "Certificate or Search" at the Registrar General's Office (RGO) presently costs $15.00 and you must supply name(s), date, and place for each event. The reason for asking for so many details on the application form is to ensure identification of the correct event. When you do not **know** all these details, you should make educated guesses or simply state "unknown". It is very important that you provide a location name, even if only a broad area like a county, and a year for the date. The fee includes a five-year search, two years on either side of the given year.

Your relationship to the party/parties of the event is requested, as well as the reason for your request, which can be stated as "genealogical" or "family history".

Application forms are available from the RGO or at AO. Make a photocopy of the blank form first for future need unless you have unlimited access to the forms.

INDEXES

Indexes to Vital Statistics in RGO custody are not open to public access so your application depends on, besides the details you've supplied, the accuracy of the clerk in the Office, not only in searching the index, but also in the transcription of the record. Two applications for a death certificate for the same person, made at different times, have been known to produce certificates with conflicting information.

Indexes were compiled by type of event, then by year, then alphabetically by surname. Marriages are indexed by both bride's and groom's names.

A **negative search notice** in lieu of the expected certificate could mean that you did not forward enough details to identify the correct registration. There may be several entries for the same name as yours. Or the event may not have been registered at the time. There is no indication on the notice of either problem. Try again when you have more information.

Under its mandate, the RGO does not exist to serve genealogists; it is clear that information given is a privilege,not a right. In late 1987, however, plans were underway to establish a genealogical department in this Office "... to provide a better service for this type of searching" according to the Deputy Registrar General. Also in 1987, a letter to the Ontario Genealogical Society from the RGO stated that possible public access to their indexes is under serious consideration.

DEATHS

Under Ontario law, death certificates do not reveal cause of death; under certain medical circumstances such information may be released. Before 1907, parents' names are normally not found on a death certificate. On other certificates you may find "not recorded" to such questions as "birthplace" or "parents" because the party or parties to the event simply left it out or did not know the answer.

Some OGS branches have been working with local funeral homes who for the most part have been very cooperative in allowing their records to be copied and indexed. These sources would be available through branch publication lists or direct enquiries to branches. **Mortuary lists** may have been published occasionally in a city directory, e.g. the 1891 directory for Toronto shows deaths during the previous year.

MUNICIPAL
OFFICES

Municipal clerks were required to keep records of vital statistics in their locality, whence came the returns to the provincial government. Not all of their copybooks have survived, but some municipal offices have them back to the 1890s. However, this has become a matter of **restricted information** within the last generation, and a local clerk is within his rights to deny these records to anyone or to confirm any information in them. While they are not truly alternative sources for vital information, some offices have been known to sympathize and offer access, perhaps due to past practice. Your request should always go to the RGO.

DIVORCE RECORDS

Strictly speaking, divorce is a court function but is included here as a relatively recent vital statistic. Since 1931 divorces have been registered at the RGO **which does not issue copies.** Filing for divorce is done in the county of residence. Needless to say, there is much sensitive information in a divorce file, most of which will not be accessible. The county court clerk can issue copies only of the original **writ** and the final decree or **judgment absolute.** The divorce itself is a Supreme Court of Ontario jurisdiction. At the Supreme Court Office in Toronto (see Appendix I) are indexed Process or Procedure Books, again chronological. These may be the only option if you do not know the county in which a divorce suit was filed. They are time-consuming and tedious to search, mainly because the books are a summary of **all** actions taken in the Supreme Court, not just divorce.

JUDGMENTS

AO now holds most Divorce Court records 1931-59 (unless space is not a problem at the local courthouse) **but** indexes to the records remain at the local courthouse. AO can also supply a copy of the **judgment** but first you must obtain the year and file number from the county court clerk, likely involving a personal visit to search the index. This index is chronological by date of filing the suit, and alphabetical by surname within each year. Information from such a document gives names of parties, their marriage date, judgment date, and possibly reference to alimony. A **writ**, and sometimes the courthouse index, will name the correspondent when adultery was the cause for divorce.

Between 1867 and 1931 divorce could only be granted by an Act of the Canadian Parliament, and information should be sought from the Clerk of the Senate, Parliament Buildings, Ottawa, Ontario K1A 0A4.

Prior to Confederation in 1867 divorce was also granted by a legislative Act, and these can be found only by checking the subject matter of Acts passed each year. The *Journals of the Proceedings of the Legislative Assembly of the Province of Canada* (26 vols.) include such indexes. *The Stuart Act of Divorce* 18 June 1841 was the first divorce to be passed by the Canadian (Canada West and Canada East) Parliament. Because of the time and expense incurred by the system before 1931, not everyone in such a situation followed the necessary official procedure. A separation agreement may have been reached, but in many cases where one partner simply vanished, it is unlikely that this step was taken. "Pioneer Divorce" by Helene Weaver in *Families*, Vol. 25, No. 2 (1986) discusses some situations like this.

ADOPTION

In Ontario, adoption records are private and closed. But recognizing the need and desire of adoptees and birth parents to seek this kind of information, the Ontario government has somewhat eased its policy. Its Adoption Disclosure Register (see Appendix I) exists to facilitate this need, but **identifying information** is only available by mutual consent of an adult adoptee and a parent who have both registered. If a birth parent has not registered, the adoptee has some recourse in that the Registry is authorized to perform searches for birth parents or other biological relatives. Consent by adoptive parents is no longer required; counselling is mandatory before identifying information is disclosed.

If a person's health, safety or welfare is at stake, the Registrar of Adoption Information may decide that disclosure is in the best interest. Anyone denied information may appeal to the Child and Family Services Review Board.

Historically, adoptions in this province would have been unofficial and unrecorded. Not until 1921 was an Adoption Law passed. The Children's Aid Society (see Appendix I) from the 1890s traditionally cared for orphans or neglected children, and found homes for many of them. While the Society still fills this role in a greatly expanded way, private adoptions have also taken place through individuals or agencies licensed by the present Ministry of Community and Social Services, under whose aegis both the Children's Aid Society and the Adoption Disclosure Registry operate.

There are finding aids at AO for the Ontario Association of Childrens' Aid Societies 1912-78, and for the Brockville Society.

MISSING
PERSONS

For this kind of contemporary searching, Idris Rogers has a useful reference article called "Searching For Lost or Missing Relatives" in *OGS Seminar Annual* (1986). City directories in the twentieth century play a major role in a hunt for birth parents, as do newspaper ads or articles for missing family. The Index to Surrogate Clerk's Application Books (see Chapter 6) can also be a great help in locating an estate file for someone, thus providing a death date.

There are also self-help groups such as Parent Finders or ALMA (Adoptees' Liberty Movement Association) that work throughout North America. Please consult local telephone directories for such addresses. "Canadian Adoptions and Discharges from Erie County, New York, Records" by Joyce S. Jewitt (*Canadian Genealogist* Vol. 7, No. 2, 1985) is a brief compilation 1876-99 that may be of interest to some searchers.

Monument in Puslinch Crown Cemetery (courtesy author)

3/ Pre-1869 Vital Statistics

1786	Major George Neal, a Methodist minister, began preaching in the Niagara area
1787	Rev. John Bethune, the first regular Presbyterian minister, in Glengarry County; construction of the Mohawk Chapel (Anglican) completed, in Brant County
1790	Lutheran church established at Williamsburg
1792	Methodist church established in Adolphustown by Rev. William Losee; Moravian missionaries in Thames Valley
1793	Marriage Act; regularization of existing unions, privilege of performing marriage extended to magistrates (only Church of England and Catholic clergy allowed, prior to this)
1797	Church of Scotland, Lutheran and Calvinist (including Baptist and Dutch Reformed) clergy allowed to perform marriages
1831	Performance of marriage confirmed for Church of Scotland, Lutheran, Presbyterian, Congregational, Independent, Tunker, Methodist, Mennonite and Moravian clergy
1858	All legitimate clergy in Upper Canada allowed to perform marriages, all to file annual returns with their County
1861	Union of Free Church and United Presbyterians to become Canada Presbyterian
1875	Union of Church of Scotland and Canada Presbyterian
1884	Methodist Church Union; New Connexion, Primitive, Wesleyan, British Wesleyan, Episcopal, Bible Christian, etc.
1925	United Church of Canada formed from union of Methodists, Congregationalists, majority of Presbyterians, smaller denominations

CHURCH
REGISTERS

When you are looking for proof of births, marriages and deaths before civil registration began, the main source is church registers in the form of baptisms, marriages and burials. In some cases birthdate is given as well as baptismal date. On the whole, burial registers were either poorly kept or are non-existent.

Finding appropriate church records for a family may be easier said than done. The procedure "from scratch" may be described as a) learning the family's location;

b) learning their religious affiliation (census is a good source); c) learning names of local churches, missions, circuits or ministers of the time period through historical reference; and d) learning if the registers still exist and where they are currently located.

Some early church records remain with the original church when it is still in use; some have been lost. In the case of a church being closed, the records may have been sent to another church in the same area or to a central church archives. Some records were part of a larger mission or circuit, so other neighbouring placenames must be noted.

To make a very generalized point, there is more chance of finding records from the larger denominations. Small denominations and congregations that died out or amalgamated with another sect may take all your powers of sleuthing to trace. In the province's earliest days, many baptisms and marriages were performed by Anglican clergy when a minister of another choice was not available.

UNITED
CHURCH

To those unfamiliar with the history of Canadian churches, we must mention that the **United Church of Canada** was a union formed in 1925 of Methodist, Congregational, the majority of Presbyterian churches, and a few small denominations. The Archives of the United Church (see Appendix I) has collected some early records for all these denominations, but some Presbyterian records will be found at PCA (see Appendix I) as well.

Although there are Methodist churches today in Ontario, they are relatively few. The Canadian Methodist Historical Society does not collect or publish church registers.

YEARBOOK

Addresses for current organized religions can be found in *Yearbook of American and Canadian Churches*, published each year by the National Council of Churches in the U.S.A., Office of Research, Evaluation and Planning, 475 Riverside Drive, New York, NY 10115.

COPIES OF
REGISTERS

Registers of many early historic churches have been microfilmed, transcribed, and/or published, and deposited at resource centres. PAC has published a *Checklist of Parish Registers* (1986) which lists church registers available there,many of which are on microfilm. AO also has a collection of registers in originals or copies, and these are arranged by town or township locations.

Baxter's *In Search of Your Roots* lists many parish registers available at central church archives, especially useful for the Anglican(Church of England) and United Church of Canada (its former component) denominations.

The LDS (Mormon) Church has microfilmed most pre-1910 Roman Catholic church registers in Ontario, with the exception of the Diocese of Hamilton and a few individual churches.

Religious denominations with archives are listed in Appendix I.

SOME
PUBLISHED/
TRANSCRIBED/
INDEXED
REGISTERS

Some church or ministers' registers available in published or transcribed form, or indexes to them, are listed here, arbitrarily arranged by counties. Full citations for books and periodicals are in Appendix II, addresses for OGS Branches are in Chapter 1, and specific reference here to other sources will be found in one of the Appendices. Some of the ministers' registers covered a wide territory, so it is best to consult neighbouring counties too. You are cautioned that, as with all transcriptions or indexes, there is always the chance of error in spelling or omission of names. Whenever possible, the **original** record is the primary, and best, evidence.

OGS = Ontario Genealogical Society (Branch)
OHS = *Ontario History* (formerly *Papers and Records of the Ontario Historical Society)*
TOR = *The Ontario Register*
JP = Justice of the Peace
RC = Roman Catholic
B = Baptisms M = Marriages D = Burials/Deaths

Brant County
M Methodist, Cainsville, 1857-69, 1879-1919, 1936-58 (Brant County OGS)
B Methodist, Cainsville, 1937-54 (Brant County OGS)
D Methodist, Cainsville, 1937-59 (Brant County OGS)

Carleton County
M RC Notre Dame Basilica, Ottawa, 1829-80 (PAC Lib)
M RC Ste. Anne, Ottawa, 1873-1900 (PAC Lib)
M RC Notre-Dame du Bon Conseil, Ottawa, 1889-1907 (PAC Lib)
M RC St-Francois d'Assise, Ottawa, 1891-1964 (PAC Lib)
M RC St-Jean-Baptiste, Ottawa, 1872-1969 (PAC Lib)
M RC Notre-Dame de Lourdes (Vanier), Ottawa, 1887-1971 (PAC Lib)

M RC St-Charles & Sacre-Coeur, Ottawa, 1910-75 (PAC Lib)
M RC Base Militaire de Fintes (Rockliffe), Ottawa, 1950-54 (PAC Lib)
BM St. Andrews Presbyterian, Ottawa, 1829-81 (*Lost in Canada*? Vol. 13, Nos. 2-4 and continued)

Elgin County
BMD Anglican, St. Thomas, 1824-30 (OHS Vol. 9)
B Anglican, Port Talbot, 1816 (TOR Vol. 6)
B Anglican, Malahide, 1858 (OHS Vol. 4)

Essex County
BMD Assumption parish, Sandwich, 1760-86 (OHS Vol. 7)
D Christ Church, Amherstburg, 1855 (TOR Vol. 4)
B Anglican, Essex & Kent, 1854-55 (TOR Vol. 7)
D 1848 (TOR Vol. 7)
M Christchurch Anglican, Detroit, Canadian people, 1849-79 (*Lost in Canada?* Vol. 3, No. 4)

Frontenac County
BMD St. Mary's Catholic, Kingston, 1816-1869 (Kingston OGS)
BM St. Andrew's Presbyterian, Kingston, 1821-69 (Kingston OGS)
BM Zion Presbyterian, Kingston, 1891-1919 (Kingston OGS)

Haldimand County
M Anglican, Rev. Cudmore Hill, 1838-59 (Hamilton OGS)
M Haldimand County 1803-56 (Norfolk Historical Society)

Halton County
M Anglican, Halton-Peel people at St. James Cathedral, Toronto, 1800-96 (Halton-Peel OGS)

Hastings County
M Hungerford 1876-1926 (Generation Press)
M Licenses 1873-86 (Belleville Library)
Kent County
M Presbyterian, Chatham, 1848-69 (TOR Vol. 4 & 6, and Kent County OGS)
B Maidstone 1857 (TOR Vol. 6)
B Methodist, Howard Circuit, 1849-50 (TOR Vol. 7)
M Harwich & vicinity, 1870-76 (Kent County OGS)
M Primitive Methodist, Chatham, 1860-83 (Kent County OGS)
BMD St. Paul's, Chatham, 1829-41 (Kent County OGS)

Lambton County
B 1838-64 (*Western Ontario Historical Notes*, Vol. 17)
B 1848-49 (TOR Vol. 4)
B Anglican, Oil Springs, 1861-63 (Lambton County OGS)
B Anglican, Forest, 1869-75 (Lambton County OGS
M Anglican, Forest, 1876 (Lambton Couty OGS)

Lanark County
M Methodist, Rideau Circuit, 1824-43 (TOR Vol. 1)
M St. Andrews 1831-65 (*Lost in Canada?* Vol. 4, #1)
B St. Andrews Presb, Perth, 1830-81 (Kingston OGS)
M St. Andrews Presb, Perth, 1830-87 (Kingston OGS)
B Scotch Church, Beckwith, 1833-51 (Ringereide's *The Flourishing Tree*)
M Scotch Church, Beckwith, 1834-51 (*The Flourishing Tree*)
BM Presb (Rev. Bell), Perth, 1817-57 (Kingston OGS)

Leeds & Grenville Counties
M Presbyterian 1812-41 (OHS Vol. 5)
BM Brockville 1814-30 (OHS Vol. 38)
B Presbyterian 1831-48 (OHS Vol. 25)

Lennox & Addington Counties
BMD Anglican, Ernestown, 1787-1814 (OHS Vol. 1 and Kingston OGS)
B Presbyterian 1800-41 (OHS Vol. 1)
BMD Presbyterian 1800-41 (Kingston OGS)
B Lutheran 1791-1850 (OHS Vol. 6)
B Presb, Napanee, 1842-1916 (Walrus Press)
M Presb, Napanee, 1853-1934 (Walrus Press)

Lincoln County
B Fort George 1821-27 (OHS Vol. 15)
BMD Anglican, Grimsby, 1817-22 (OHS Vol. 3)
M JP, Grimsby, 1796-1822 (Powell's *Annals of the Forty*, Vol. 1)
M Anglican, Grimsby, 1823-50 (*Annals of the Forty*, Vol. 10)
BMD Anglican, St. Catharines, 1791-1827 (Ker's *St. George's Parish Church, St. Catharines*)
BM St. Mark's Anglican, Newark, 1781-1834 (OHS Vol. 3)
BMD St. Mark's Anglican, Newark, 1792-1850 (OHS Vol. 3)
B St. Mark's, Niagara, 1832-40 (TOR Vol. 6 & 7)
B Presbyterian, Newark, 1795-1814 (OHS Vol. 3)
M Queenston 1825-38 (TOR Vol. 6 & 7)
B Presbyterian, Clinton, 1824-34 (*Families* Vol. 27, No. 1)

Middlesex County
M Presbyterian 1833-49 (*Families*, Vol. 10, No. 4)
M Methodist 1839-51 (TOR Vol. 6)
M St. Paul's Anglican, London, 1829-34 (*Lost in Canada?* Vol. 4, No. 3)

Norfolk County
BMD St. John's Anglican, Woodhouse, 1830-39 and 1838-51 (*Western Ontario Historical Notes* May & Dec 1968)
BMD St. John's Anglican, Woodhouse, 1830-1948 (Norfolk Historical Society)
BMD St. Paul's Presbyterian, Simcoe, 1849-1900 (Norfolk Historical Society)
M Baptist, Woodhouse, 1831-57 (TOR Vol. 4)
M JP 1810-28 (TOR Vol. 4)
M Norfolk County 1795-1870 (Norfolk Historical Society)

Northumberland County
M Rev. Neil, Seymour, 1840-78 (Quinte OGS)
B Rev. Neil, Seymour, 1852-72 (Quinte OGS)

Oxford County
BMD 1839-51 (Oxford County OGS)
M Presbyterian, Ingersoll, 1847-57 (Oxford County OGS)

Peel County
BMD Christ Church Anglican, Brampton, 1851-70, index (*People of Peel*)
B Mission for Chingacousy, Toronto Gore, and other places 1843-57 (*People of Peel*)

Perth County
M Presbyterian, Stratford Knox, 1850-57 (Perth County OGS)
B Anglican, Stratford, 1852-64 (Waterloo-Wellington OGS)

Peterborough County
B Anglican, Lakefield, 1857-58 (TOR Vol. 6)
B Catholic, Peterborough, 1855 (TOR Vol. 6)
D Methodist, Asphodel, 1857 (TOR Vol. 7)

Prince Edward County
M JP 1803-22 (OHS Vol. 1, & Generation Press)
B Methodist, Picton, 1811-37 (TOR Vol. 3)
M Methodist, Picton, 1831-57 (TOR Vol. 4)
BM Methodist Episcopal circuit, 1805-53 (Quinte Branch, UEL Association)
M Bay of Quinte, 1836-38 (Generation Press)

Simcoe County
M St. James Anglican, Orillia, 1841-57 (Simcoe County OGS)
M Anglican, Simcoe people at St. James Cathedral, Toronto, 1800-96 (Simcoe County OGS)
M Presbyterian, Simcoe people at St. Andrews, Toronto, (Simcoe County OGS)

Stormont, Dundas & Glengarry Counties
B Methodist 1859 (TOR Vol. 4)
B Methodist Episcopal, Winchester, 1865 (TOR Vol. 4)
BMD Presbyterian, St. Andrews West, 1804-56 Leeds & (Grenville OGS)
BM Presbyterian, Lochiel, 1820-84 (Leeds & Grenville OGS)
B Methodist, 1878-1903 (Glengarry Genealogical Society)
M Methodist, 1879-99 (Glengarry Genealogical Society)
B Hepzibah Church, 1899-1911 (Glengarry Genealogical Society)
M Hepzibah Church, 1899-1910 (Glengarry Genealogical Society)
BMD St. Raphael's RC, from 1804 (Glengarry Genealogical Society)
BMD St. Finnan's RC, from 1833 (Glengarry Genealogical Society)
BMD St. Andrew's, Williamstown, from 1779 (Glengarry Genealogical Society)
M Trinity Anglican, Cornwall, 1803-45 (*Lost in Canada?*, Vol. 5, No. 2; Vol. 6, No. 3)
BM Presb, Rev. John Bethune, 1779-1810 (*Lost in Canada?* Vol. 11, No. 3)

Victoria County
D 1870-71 (TOR Vol. 6 & 7)

Waterloo County
BD Lutheran, Kitchener, 1833-35 (TOR Vol. 1)
M 1866 (OGS *Bulletin* Vol. 1)
B St. John's Anglican, Kitchener, 1848-74 (Waterloo-Wellington OGS)
M St. John's Anglican, Kitchener, 1878-89 (Waterloo-wellington OGS)
D St. John's Anglican, Kitchener, 1849-90 (Waterloo-Wellington OGS)
D Trinity Anglican, Galt, 1851-74 (Waterloo-Wellington OGS)
BMD Lutheran, Plattsville, 1865-1904 (Waterloo-Wellington OGS)
BMD Lutheran, Strasburg, 1844-93 (Waterloo-Wellington OGS)

B Waterloo County 1872-73 (Waterloo-Wellington OGS)

D Waterloo County 1870-72 (Waterloo-Wellington OGS)

Welland County

BMD St. Paul's Anglican, Fort Erie, 1836-44 (OHS Vol. 27)

M St. Paul's Anglican, Fort Erie, 1844-70 (TOR Vol. 1)

B St. Paul's Anglican, Fort Erie, 1844-52 (TOR Vols. 1 & 2)

D St. Paul's, Fort Erie, 1844-50 (TOR Vol. 2)

M Anglican, Chippawa, 1820-35 (OHS Vol. 8)

BD Anglican, Chippawa, 1820-37 (OHS Vol. 8)

M Presbyterian, Stamford, 1827-34 (OHS Vol. 8)

M Quaker, Pelham, 1800-42 (TOR Vol. 4)

M JP, Chippawa, 1801-12, 1816-32 (OHS Vol. 8)

M All Saints, Niagara Falls, 1885-1902 (TOR Vol. 4)

Wellington County

M Presbyterian, Puslinch, 1840-57 (TOR Vol. 4 & 6)

M Eramosa, 1858-82 (Guelph Public Library)

BD St. George's Anglican, Harriston, 1858-75 (Waterloo-Wellington OGS)

BMD Anglican, North Arthur, 1858-62 (Waterloo-Wellington OGS)

M Baptist, Erin, 1858-75 (Wellington County Archives)

M Baptist/Disciples, Eramosa/Niagara, 1828-42 (Wellington County Archives)

Wentworth County

BMD Ancaster 1830-38 (OHS Vol. 5)

BM Anglican 1816-27 (OHS Vol. 5)

M Presbyterian 1848-56 (*Lost in Canada?* Vol. 5, No. 1)

M W. Flamborough 1817-32 (Waterdown Heritage Society)

York County

M St. James Anglican Cathedral, Toronto, 1800-96, indexed (Toronto OGS)

M St. James Cathedral, Toronto, 1800-96 (Robertson's *Landmarks of Toronto* Vol. 3 *)

B St. James Cathedral, Toronto, 1807-70 (Robertson's *Landmarks of Toronto* Vol. 3 & 4 *)

M Congregational, Richmond Hill, 1819-43 (OHS Vol. 27)

M Knox Presbyterian, Toronto, 1826-29 (*York Pioner* 1960)

M Presbyterian, Toronto, 1841-54 (TOR Vol. 4)

M Quaker, Yonge Street, 1804-40 (TOR Vol. 4)

M Toronto 1806-09 (TOR Vol. 2)

M Catholic 1830-33 (TOR Vol. 7)

* Considerable errors and misinterpretations occurred in Robertson's *Landmarks*. The North York Historical Society has compiled many corrections to this over the years since its publication.

FINDING
AIDS

There is no easy way to deal with locating the register you need. Check catalogues of PAC, AO and OGS branches or correspond with the minister of an individual church. Most large denominations publish an annual report, directory or yearbook with names and addresses of churches. In years to come, the OGS *Inventory of Church Registers* will be the standard reference work for researchers in this field. It is expected that the first volume of this project will be published after 1990.

Meanwhile, some local guides are available, besides archival or institutional catalogues, such as *Reference Guide to RC Parishes, Diocese of Peterborough* (Kawartha OGS), *Church Directory For the County of Brant* (Brant OGS), *Diocese of Ontario (Anglican Church of Canada): Archives, Preliminary Inventory* and *A Checklist of Pre-1900 Baptist, Methodist, Presbyterian, and United churches in Waterloo & Wellington Counties* (Waterloo-Wellington OGS).

It should be remembered that church records, once you have found what you want, consist of much more than baptismal, marriage and burial entries. In the absence of some of these, or in addition to them, you may find valuable references in membership or communion rolls, meeting minutes, and other records if accessible.

CORRESPONDING

Please do not expect a minister/priest/church officer to give you free search time for your ancestors. Always enclose a token money order as a goodwill gesture with your stamped, self-addressed envelope. Also, **only** Canadian stamps can be used in Canada; otherwise use International Postal Reply Coupons. Most churches or denominational archives do not have the staff to handle requests by mail, although they may indicate whether the records you want are there.

For more description of the holdings in church archives of various denominations(Catholic, Anglican, United, Presbyterian, and Baptist) see *Readings in Ontario Genealogical Sources.*

For listings of various denominations that practised in Ontario through the years, mainly nineteenth century, see Chapter 4.

Recommended articles:

--"Utility and Variety of Early Church Records" by Bruce Elliott in *Families*, Vol. 16, No. 4 (1977)

--"The Use of Quaker Records and Minutes for Genealogical Search in Ontario" by Jane Zavitz in *Families*, Vol. 19, No. 1 (1980), in conjunction with the Quaker records and finding aid (at University of Western Ontario in London, AO and PAC, originals at Pickering College, Newmarket)

--"Roman Catholic History and Archives in Ontario" by Fr. Robert J. Scollard in *Families*, Vol. 13, No. 2 (1974)

--"Genealogical Sources in the Catholic Archdiocese of Toronto You May Have Overlooked" by J.L. Bulger in *Families*, Vol. 24, No. 1 (1985)

--"Where the Friends Were/Are" by Harold Zavitz in OGS *Bulletin*, Vol. 9, No. 3 (1970) which consists mainly of a wonderful map of Quaker settlements and cemeteries.

--"The Early Years of the Tunkers in Upper Canada" by E. Morris Sider in *Ontario History*, Vol. 51, No. 2 (1959)

CEMETERIES

Cemetery inscriptions can provide evidence that may not be found elsewhere - date of death, age at death, and sometimes, fortuitously, place of birth. To begin with, you must know where your ancestor lived (and died), and learn where the local cemeteries are.

However it may not be necessary to visit the actual site. First you should check whatever transcriptions have been made, through one of the three main repositories where all completed OGS transcriptions are deposited. Many OGS branches have now transcribed all cemeteries in their county or region. AO has microfilmed everything that was submitted up to about the fall of 1986, as of this publication date, and microfilming this series is a priority with the Archives. Also, a local OGS branch will sell its transcriptions for a nominal charge.

The drawbacks are that the headstone that you seek may have succumbed to years of weathering; and we are dealing with secondary evidence to a certain extent. Certainly the date of death would be primary evidence, normally supplied by a relative who had been nearby when death occurred. But that same relative, whether widow(er) or child, may not have had true knowledge of the deceased's age and place of birth, especially if the latter was in a country unfamiliar to the informant. Needless to say, your information is dependent on the accuracy and skill of the transcriber, so finding the original headstone may be one of your goals.

VARIOUS SOURCES	A transcription of a headstone in a cemetery is not quite the same thing as a cemetery burial register, or a plot owners' list. These too, along with cemetery maps or burial plans, may be useful. Just be sure you distinguish in your own records what the actual source was, and that there is no confusion between a death date and a burial date. Occasionally information from a church burial register may differ from that on a headstone or in a cemetery office register. When there is conflict or doubt, all available sources will have to be checked, not only for accuracy of the death date, but for the pursuit of a possible obituary. You will often find that when custody of some cemeteries was taken over by local citizens' or municipal boards, burial registers begin only from the date of their management.

The Ontario Association of Cemeteries (Appendix I) publishes *Directory of Member Cemeteries*, with names and addresses arranged alphabetically by town or community. Toronto Trust Cemeteries, 48 St. Clair West, 9th Floor, Toronto M4V 2Z2 administers a variety of burial grounds, and will answer queries or allow access to record books. See "Records and Resources of Toronto Trust Cemeteries" by Marcia Darling in *OGS Seminar Annual* (1985). |
| OBITUARIES | Looking for an obituary is a natural adjunct to finding a death date. If a local newspaper exists for that date, you may find a published tribute. This seems to occur more frequently when the deceased was a pioneer or a prominent citizen. The best obituaries often mention previous origins, arrival here, occupation, community involvement, surviving family and their locations. Other times you may find only a simple death notice, possibly with place of interment.

A word of advice for the eager but unwary obituary searcher: the tendency quite often is to scan each issue of a newspaper for the Births/Marriages/Deaths column. Those who are unsuccessful in finding a death notice may not realize that some deaths were reported elsewhere in the newspaper and did not make the notices column. Read the **entire newspaper** for your surname. Obituaries and death notices are often found among news items or especially in columns devoted to rural areas surrounding the town of publication. |
| NEWSPAPER NOTICES | As mentioned in the Introduction concerning **indexes**, Hunterdon House has published many volumes of BMD notice from early newspapers. Volume 5 of *The Ontario Register* is also mainly devoted to newspaper notices, and some appear as well in most other volumes. There is an excellent source to consult in this regard: |

Gilchrist's *Inventory of Ontario Newspapers 1793-1986, First Edition 1987.* In an alphabetical arrangement by placename the book shows dates of all newspapers which have ever existed, where to locate them, and which ones have been indexed for vital statistics notices.

Both AO and PAC have fine collections of nineteenth and twentieth century newspapers for southern Ontario. Many local libraries, OGS branches, and individual researchers are also involved in newspaper indexing projects. Often a local library or archives houses the old original newspaper editions for their areas, and have been responsible for their microfilming and thus wider access through Inter Library Loan.

Major religions started denominational newspapers and periodicals which regularly featured birth, marriage and death notices or obituaries. Some notable examples are:
--Wesleyan Methodist **Christian Guardian** (at AO and UCA from 1829, nominal index at UCA for early years)
--**Catholic Register** (RCA, AO from 1893, not indexed)
--**Catholic Record** (AO from 1878, not indexed)
--**Christian Messenger** later called **Canadian Baptist** (CBA from 1854, indexed by Hamilton Branch OGS to 1873)
--Anglican **Canadian Churchman** (AO from 1876, not indexed)
--**Presbyterian Record** (at PCA from 1844, not indexed).

METHODIST
BAPTISMAL
REGISTERS

From the 1840s Wesleyan Methodist ministers were required by their church to submit baptismal returns, which were copied into a central register. This is a case where the register is a **second** copy of the minister's first record. Arranged by township, town or city up until the 1890s, these entries can prove to be a real treasure. Generally they show name of the child, date and place of birth and baptism, parents' names and residence, and name of minister.

The pages of these registers, as you read them in order of entry, are not necessarily in chronological order. They must be viewed personally at the UCA on microfilm. There is a finding aid for placenames.

It is believed that most other Methodists did not follow this practice. However a register for **Methodist Episcopal** baptisms, Niagara Conference, 1858-84, is also available at UCA. This one, unfortunately, does not give parents' residence at the time of baptism, although

To All Whome it may concern this may certify that Egbert McLees
and Ann Rony were joined together in Holy Matrimony by me a Minister
of the Methodist Episcopal Church in Upper Canada the 2 day of January
in the year of our Lord one thousand Eight hundred and 43 by the authority
of Being published as made and provided by the Statutes given under my
hand the day and year above written in presence of   signed Barney Markle
signed Abraham Pike   Minister of the Methodist Episcopal
signed Eli Woodrow   Church in U C

                                                        Signed

---

List of Marriages Solemnized by me Edward Topping a Minister of the Baptist
Denomination in Oxford West in the county of Oxford the District of Brock and in
the Province of Canada from the thirtieth day of November in the year of our Lord
one thousand eight hundred and forty two to the same day of November in 1843
both days inclusive

Day of Month	Year	Names of Persons	Township	Names of Witnesses	License or Banns
Nov 30	1842	John Nunn / Rachel Pearl	Both of Zorra	William Rowel / John Beaford	By Banns
January 23	1843	James Sim / Elizabeth Adams	Both of Blandford	William Bell / Colin McLean	By Banns
Jan 26	1843	Benjamin Honor / Disera Charles	Both of Blenheim	James Akins / Henry E Horna	By License
Feb 21	1843	John Charles / Susan Adelaide Taylor	Both of Blenheim	Jordon Charles / Henry E Horna	By License
October 23	1843	Nathaniel Bell / Mary Livingston	Both of Woodstock	Mary James / Ann Eliza Jones	By License
Oct 25	1843	Richard J Kidd / Elena Cusins	of Blandford / of Burford	James Dow / George Beamer	By License
Oct 21	1843	Laura M Elliott / Sally Ann Hadwell	of Oxford West / of Norwich	Joseph L Cook / Daniel Hadwell	Banns

                Signed   Edward Topping
                      Minister of the First Baptist Church in
                                Blenheim.

Entry from Brock District Marriage Register, RG 8, I-6-A, Vol. 2 (courtesy Archives of Ontario) date and place of the child's birth is shown. They are not chronological entries as such, but rather each minister's entire series is entered all at once.

DISTRICT
MARRIAGE
REGISTERS

District Marriage Registers were created by District Clerks of the Peace from 1793 but early entries were few, made only if the couple paid to enter a copy of their marriage certificate. After 1831 this form of civil registration was compulsory for "dissenting" denominations which had been given the right to perform marriages that year. Anglican and Catholic clergy were exempt from providing these returns, or copies, to a District Clerk.

Surviving Registers begin at different dates and generally continue until 1858 when county registers were established. To use a District Register, and most are indexed, you must know your location and then determine which district covered the area.

The following District Registers are available at AO on microfilm (there is a finding aid filed under **Department of the Provincial Secretary, Appendix F):**

Bathurst	London
Brock	Newcastle
Colborne	Ottawa
Gore	Prince Edward
Home	Talbot
Huron	Victoria
Johnstown	

Western and Eastern District Registers have been published in *The Ontario Register*, Vols. 1-4. Many other District Registers were serialized beginning in Vol. 6. Entirely missing in original form are those for Midland and Niagara Districts, and some "newer" districts as Wellington, Simcoe and Dalhousie. Information contained in the Registers is minimal -- names of parties, place and date of marriage, denomination and witnesses.

INDEXES

A few notes about using the microfilmed original registers are in order here. The indexes are, of course, handwritten, and some are more legible than others. Look for indexing that is continued (because of inadequate page room) at the back or front of a register, "overflow" entries that continue under initials that don't have many entries *per se* (sometimes you will see "continued under such-and-such initial"), whether the index includes both brides' and grooms' names, and whether occasionally first and last names have been reversed,

41

Return   *Kenneth Maclennan*   *for 1861*

BRIDEGROOM.						
NAME.	AGE.	RESIDENCE.	PLACE OF BIRTH.	NAMES OF PARENTS.	NAME.	AGE.
James Keith	24	Pickering	Aberdeen	Alexander Keith Mary Mitchell	Jean Paterson	22
Alexander McIntosh	30	Pickering	Nairnshire	Wm McIntosh Eliza Ross	Anne Gowlie	36
Thomas Stephenson	21	Pickering	Pickering	Thomas Stephenson Mary Matthew	Rachel Hood	21
George Harris	38	Whitby	England	Henry Harris Sarah Boland	Mary Ann Britton	29

I hereby certify that the foregoing is a true and correct Statement of all Marriages preceding the date hereof

Whitby Jany 1st 1862.

Entry from Ontario County Marriage Register, RG 8, I-6-B, Vol. 45 (courtesy Archives of Ontario, RG 8)

which is tricky if your eye is watching only the margin column.

COUNTY MARRIAGE REGISTERS

County Marriage Registers began in 1858, no longer based on the obsolete district, and continued until civil registration began in 1869. Some continue to a later date, and some have the occasional birth register. These registers include marriages of **all** denominations.

INDEXES

A series of indexes to these is being published by Generation Press (see Appendix II) with the warning that the Registers themselves are **second copies** of the original records, so that indexing was actually done as a third transcription. Obviously this leaves room for error, beginning with the minister when he made the original entry, and when he made copies for the government at the end of each year. There are currently seventeen published indexes.

There is more information here than in District Registers -- names and ages of parties, residence, birthplace, parents' names (often the mother's birth surname), date and place of marriage, denomination, and witnesses. AO holds the original registers and microfilmed copies, and the same finding aid applies as above.

Filed 9th January 1862   *N° 17885.*

	BRIDE.			WITNESS.		DATE OF
	RESIDENCE.	PLACE OF BIRTH.	NAMES OF PARENTS.	NAME.	RESIDENCE.	MARRIAGE.
2	Whitby	Aberdeen	John Paterson Margaret Campbell	Alexander Keith John Keith	Whitby	Jany 3rd
3	Pickering	Berwickshire	William Donlin Isabella Henderson	George Donlin	Pickering	April 3rd
1	Pickering	Whitchurch	Francis Hood Edmy Gould	Mattey Wilson Ellen Stephinson	Pickering	May 8th
4	Whitby	England	George Britton Sarah Harris	George Britton Edward Harris	Whitby	Decr 13th

... solemnized by one for the year ending on the 31st day of December next

½d

L. Maclennan Min St. Andrews Church
Whitby Ont.

JUSTICE
OF THE
PEACE

A few further comments can be made before we leave vital statistics. A marriage not found in local church records nor in the above registers, may have been performed by a **Justice of the Peace.** Some are found in pre-1831 District Registers if the couple paid the registration fee; after 1831 there are fewer found in district Registers. The odd collection of such records may be found in main repositories catalogued under "Marriage Records" or geographical placename material. Also, please refer to the lengthy list of published records earlier in this chapter.

In the earliest days of the province only the Church of England and the Roman Catholic Church were authorized to perform marriages. In a District with less than five Anglican clergymen, a Justice of the Peace was allowed to marry couples who lived more than eighteen miles from the nearest clergyman. Gradually other denominations were "recognized", many not until 1831 or later. Some of these performed their own marriage rites before this, and the Marriage Act of 1858 "legalized" them. When you reach a dead end for a marriage source, it is always wise to look at Anglican registers for the area.

BONDS,
LICENCES

Marriage bonds record the names of parties who obtained a marriage licence rather than being married after

43

publication of banns in a church. The couple had some friends sign the bond, agreeing to pay a penalty if any legal impediment to the proposed marriage was later discovered. A collection 1803-45 is indexed, available at both PAC and AO. The bond will tell names of the parties **intending** to marry, residence, date and place of bond, bondsmen, and sometimes a witness. You cannot always assume that a marriage followed. Also, **not** every marriage by licence will be included in this series. Wilson's *Marriage Bonds of Ontario 1803-1834* is abstracted from this series.

The Ontario Archives also has some collections of individuals' marriage licences 1853-1911; the "Marriages" finding aid has a surname index.

Sample of old handwritten indexes, Home District Marriage Register, RG 8, I-6-A, Vol. 10 (courtesy Archives of Ontario)

4/ Census Returns

1842	Province-wide census, heads of households only
1851/2	First census to name all household members, enumerated January **1852**
1861	Census enumerated 14 August
1871	Census enumerated 2 April
1881	Census enumerated 4 April
1891	Census enumerated 6 April
1901	Census to be released in 2001, possibly earlier

Finding ancestors in census returns helps to fill out your family groups and sometimes adds a generation. The **personal** schedules of the census provide the most valuable information for the genealogist. Here you will learn of their religious affiliation which will help in searching out church records. When you have found your family, do not stop at that page. You might as well finish the entire town or township for other surname occurrences, because you never know when you might find another family a little farther on. Of course the record will not specify relationships between families; you'll have to seek other proof. Other schedules of the census are also of interest, but are available only for 1851 to 1871.

"OTHER"
CENSUSES

Before 1842 a census was taken annually by township assessors and filed with the local District Clerk of the Peace. Few of these have survived, and they have little information other than helping you establish a residence for a head of household at a certain date. Some that survived are listed as municipal records in Chapter 8 with names of places. Those that came into PAC custody are accessible through the major census finding aid called *Census Returns 1666-1891*. Odd **fragments** of census returns collected by PAC are listed in their finding aid 300, available from PAC's Public Service Section.

1848-1850

A widely available index in microfiche form to 1848 and 1850 census returns has been quite misleading to many researchers unfamiliar with Ontario's earlier political boundaries. At the time of these census enumerations, there were nineteen districts in Ontario. This index is for the **only three surviving district returns,** i.e. Huron, Johnstown and Newcastle. Fragments have also survived for a few counties outside these districts. Any index is useful as long as its limitations are understood. In this case, this is definitely not a comprehensive index to Ontario residents for those years.

Returns for areas apart from the above may have been located and preserved by a regional repository. For instance, the 1848 census for Norfolk County is in the custody of the Norfolk Historical Society.

For the most part we are concerned here with the more complete census returns from 1842 to 1891, and 1901 when it becomes available. **Census returns after 1901** are unlikely ever to be released to the custody of the PAC for public access, because of the sworn confidentiality under which enumeration was made. The 1901 census may be released somewhat earlier than the year 2001, depending on the prevailing government's right to privacy policy. **Maps of enumeration districts** have not survived. Boundaries for the wards in large towns and cities may be ascertained from a contemporary directory.

FINDING
AID

Ontario Census Returns, the finding aid we will refer to, is your guide to the microfilm reels, and it (alphabetically arranged by town and township name) should be available at the repository where you view the films. In fact this finding aid is simply the Ontario portion of PAC's *Census Returns 1666-1891* which can be purchased through the federal government's Supply and Services Canada (Appendix I).

There are occasional "miscellaneous" entries in the finding aid that could easily be overlooked. Under **"Institutions"** in the 1891 census there are sub-headings for various counties. These returns are enumerations for the most part of county charitable homes and hospitals, those institutions for the needy, aged and homeless. Chapter 12 addresses these situations in a little more detail. The difficulty in trying to identify an ancestor here is that rarely are surnames ever shown. Other miscellaneous headings are **Indian Reserves** (Lambton County in 1861), **Ojibwa Indian** (Middlesex County in 1851) and **Grand River Tract** (Haldimand-Brant Counties 1816-1832).

INDEXES

The OGS *Index to the 1871 Census of Ontario* is becoming the most important tool for locating Ontario residents just after Confederation took place. The Index is not entirely available yet but the volumes (by county or groups of counties) are being published as quickly as possible. Every head of household and "stray" is included, along with some identifying information to lead you to the appropriate original return.

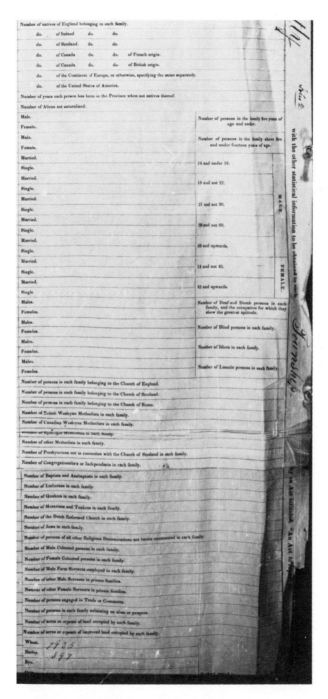

Headings from 1842 census, Huntly township, Bathurst District, reel C-1344 (courtesy National Archives of Canada)

Another useful publication from OGS is Crowder's *Indexes to Ontario Census Records* which lists alphabetically by placename all those returns that have nominal indexes, compiled by various sources.

It is vital to remember that we do not know who gave the information to the enumerator. The informant may not have been the head of the family, so certainly some guessing at information and some deliberate misinformation happened. Also you cannot assume that a family that appears in "part one" or "district one" in one census year will appear in the same part every year.

1842

Returns for 1842 named heads of households only, but they included age statistics on family members, birthplaces, religion and agricultural information, if the enumerator filled in every column (see illustration). In *Ontario Census Returns* the 1842 census is shown under **county** or **district** names, which doesn't tell you if a certain township within that area is available. You will find on viewing the microfilms that a few townships have aggregates (statistics) only. Not all townships were settled or organized enough to take a census in 1842, and not every return originally taken has survived. Occasionally a township will be shown in the finding aid with an 1842 listing. These relate to returns separately filmed for the Gore and Niagara Districts. These are described further in Chapter 8 as mentioned above.

Because you can't tell from the finding aid just which townships are available in each county, this is a list of townships that are available according to the inventory on the microfilm reels. Counties not listed mean there are no surviving returns.

1842 Census Returns

County	Township
Leeds & Grenville	Augusta, S. Gower, Wolford, Yonge, front & rear Leeds & Lansdowne, Kitley, Elizabethtown, S. & N. Crosby, Bastard
Carleton	Goulbourn, Nepean, Huntley, Fitzroy, Torbolton
Lanark	Beckwith, Bathurst, Dalhousie, Darling, Drummond, Lanark, Lavant, Pakenham, N. & S. Sherbrooke
Renfrew	Horton, Westmeath, Ross, McNab
Frontenac	Kingston Ward 4
Northumberland	Hamilton, Haldimand, Cramahe, Murray, Seymour, Percy, Monaghan

Durham	Clarke, Darlington, Manvers, Cartwright
York	Toronto 5 Wards
Lincoln	Clinton, Gainsborough
Welland	Niagara (Town), Niagara, Stamford, Thorold, Wainfleet, Willoughby
Haldimand	Canborough, Cayuga, Rainham, Walpole
Halton	Trafalgar, Esquesing
Wentworth	Hamilton, Barton
Brant	Brantford Indian Reserve
Middlesex	Adelaide, Caradoc, Delaware, N. Dorchester, Ekfrid, Lobo, Mosa, Westminster, London (Town), London
Elgin	Aldborough, Dunwich, Southwold, Yarmouth, Malahide, Bayham, S. Dorchester
Huron	Ashfield, Wawanosh

1851-1881

Even areas of the 1851 census have not survived; an unfortunate example is Toronto and much of York County. From this date the census named all members of a household with age, place of birth, occupation, religious affiliation, marital status, and in 1871 and 1881, a column for **origin** which indicated the ethnic heritage of the father of each person. As an example of how this column can help identify people, in one family the husband's origin was English, the wife's Irish, the two older children French, and remaining children English. This helped confirm family tradition that the wife had been previously married to a French Canadian, and had children by him.

As with the 1842 returns, those for 1851 can be difficult to read, and page numbers may have been arbitrarily designated during the microfilming process. If pages were assembled out of order, a family may continue on a second sheet not following the first one. Some enumerators were under-supplied with government forms and had to improvise forms to their chagrin, and these may be even more difficult to read than the official ones. Robert E. Paterson in North Easthope in 1852 was prompted to observe in his report, "I have no remarks to make but if ever you should make me enumerator again I hope you will send me more paper."

ENUMERATORS' REMARKS

Otherwise, most enumerators provided a little more local colour in their reports. Look for these reports with early census returns, sometimes at the beginning, sometimes at the end of the personal schedules. Some have added notes in the right hand columns about a particular business or building. And some have even singled out

49

individuals in their specific districts. In St. Lawrence Ward of the 1861 return for Toronto, the enumerator was so impressed with the "oldest person in my division", Mr. Edward Leary, that he supplied a long note about the man's age, birthplace, emigration date and various occupations, ending with "He retains all his mental faculties save a little want of hearing, and can walk four to five miles daily at a smart pace." Instructions to enumerators 1871-91 are on microfiche at the National Library and can be borrowed through Inter Library Loan.

Another "flaw" among the 1851 returns is that **parts** of one census may be missing, and this may not be shown in the finding aid. For example, for Clarke township, only district four of the agricultural schedule is microfilmed. Make sure you record all headings of what you are reading, note whether all parts or census districts seem to be included, and whether gaps or ommissions have occurred.

Some institutions that hold copies of the 1871 Census personal schedule, do not have the accompanying seven schedules which were filmed later. Besides the mention below of deaths and agricultural schedules, the others can supply such information as local commercial and industrial establishments with names of owners, product or service, and number of employees.

The personal schedule **only** for 1881 was microfilmed. There are no remaining schedules in existence now. In fact, the personal schedule for 1881 was destroyed after filming, and the 1881 census is known for poor film quality. Many pages and even entire townships are illegible, overexposed or out of focus.

1891

Again, only the personal schedule was filmed, and no other schedules remain. A column was added in this census that shows each householder's relationship to the head. An "L" designation seems to mean a non-family member, but there is no extant explanation of this. Another addition of genealogical benefit in this census was the request for birthplace of both parents of each person. Pages of this census may also be found out of order. Returns for some townships are totally or partially missing, especially in Wellington County, and these are indicated as such in the finding aid.

By 1891, census districts no longer necessarily conformed to geographical county boundaries. See notes on Bothwell, Cardwell and Monck, below.

For ancestors that lived in a large town or city in these later census returns, a street directory near the census date can shorten your search. With the address, you can determine from the directory the exact **ward** the family lived in. This applies mainly to Toronto, Hamilton, London, Ottawa, Brockville and Kingston.

1901

Government policy has been to release the past few census returns 92 years after the census year. However we cannot assume this will also be the case for the 1901 census. We can only say that 1993 might be the earliest we may see it, or we may have to wait until 2001. The most important addition to this return for genealogists is the column asking for year of emigration to Canada.

BOTHWELL, CARDWELL, MONCK

In the 1871 and 1881 census, three "artificial" counties were created for enumeration purposes only. Each of them "took" towns and townships from more than one county. This is only confusing if a researcher tries to find these names on a map because they will not be shown as counties. Townships and towns or villages included in each are as follows, with their "real" county location in brackets:

BOTHWELL

Bothwell village (Kent)	Orford (Kent)
Camden (Kent)	Ridgetown village (Kent)
Dawn (Lambton)	Sombra (Lambton)
Dresden village (Kent)	Thamesville village (Kent)
Euphemia (Lambton)	Zone (Kent)
Howard (Kent)	

CARDWELL

Adjala (Simcoe)	Caledon (Peel)
Albion (Peel)	Mono (Dufferin)
Bolton village (Peel)	

MONCK

Caistor (Lincoln)	Moulton (Haldimand)
Canborough (Haldimand)	Pelham (Welland)
Dunn (Haldimand)	Sherbrooke (Haldimand)
Dunnville village (Haldimand)	Wainfleet (Welland)
Gainsborough (Lincoln)	

NAMES

We expect names on a census to be quite reliable. But there are two points to watch for and examine. **Surnames** as has been mentioned earlier may vary from the spelling you know. The enumerator has been known to exercise wild licence in his spelling of a name, and phonetic sounding is usually the key. You need to compare names of children, ages, birthplaces, etc. to make

51

a conclusion. **First names** can be obscured by the use of nicknames, e.g. "Nancy" for Ann, "Minnie" for Melinda or Wilhelmina, "Sally" for Sarah, and numerous other variations. A child may have been known by his or her second name, and so may be listed in a census by either one in different years.

There have been odd occasions of two census enumerations. These seem to occur in such circumstances as when a child is away from home at school or working. His parents may have listed him, which technically was "wrong" if he did not spend the enumeration night at home, and his employer or boarding house or boarding school may have listed him as well. The same thing has occurred when part of the family was away visiting. Someone at home listed them, and the host head of family did the same. This sort of thing may only be found by accident, unless you know exactly where a missing family member might have been at that time. If you run across an occurrence like this, it is interesting to note any discrepancies, and to evaluate which source would be most reliable.

AGE

Age is commonly faulty information on a census return. In 1851 and 1861 the question was **age at next birthday**. Because the 1851 census was taken in January 1852, the great majority of people were giving their age for that year. It is almost a rule that the earliest census return in which an ancestor appears is more reliable for age than when he became older. In other words, the younger he is the less reason there is for parents to get sloppy with dates, or for himself to add or subtract a few years. "Records Can Be Deceiving: Problems with Pinpointing Birth Dates in Nineteenth Century Ontario Sources" by Larry Noonan in *Families*, Vol. 26, No. 2 (1987) takes a detailed look at this.

Your goal is to use ages to determine birth dates. But primary evidence of age or birth date will have to be found elsewhere. By the 1871 census, **present age** was requested.

BIRTHPLACE

The informant may not have known place of birth for all members of the family or household, so again, some information may be guessing. Some abbreviations used for birthplace in Ontario are:

O. (Ontario)   U.C. (Upper Canada)
C.W. (Canada West)   E.C. (English Canada)

Birthplace referred to as **"F"** in 1851 does **not** mean "foreign born"; it generally refers to "French", and in this context infers French-Canadian. Strangely enough,

"F" can also indicate "of British parentage", as reported by a census enumerator in the 1851 census of Camden East. Another enumerator in Richmond stated that his "F" referred to foreign born **parents** of the person in question! Enumerators' instructions for 1851 have never been found, so interpretation becomes an individual matter.

My experience is that enumerators sometimes became carried away with their ditto marks, those ubiquitous "Do." entries on line after line. Perhaps they lost track of which line they were on, or it was easier to make the mark than to enter a different birthplace or religion for some family members. Check birthplaces of children against those of parents. A husband born in Scotland and a wife born in Germany were unlikely to have had children born in Germany.

When the first child or children were born outside Canada, you might infer two things: that the marriage probably took place there, not in Canada, and that the time period between the last child born outside Canada, and the first child born here, indicates the date of emigration or arrival.

RELIGION

Religious affiliation can be considered accurate information; watch for a wife's differing from her husband's. To find their church marriage record you should look for both religious sources, favouring the wife's since usually the marriage took place in her local church or parish. You may notice a change in affiliation from one census year to another which could affect children's baptisms. Most frustrating is the family that lists "No Creed" or "None" for the religion column. The only hope is to locate an older generation, or the same family in an earlier return, still affiliated with an organized religion. If they resided in the same area for some time prior to this, then you can investigate local histories and narrow down the possibilities from churches that existed then.

RELIGIOUS ABBREVIATIONS

Many entries in the religion column are self-explanatory, but some abbreviations used are as follows. There are quite a few additional small religions that flourished in pockets here and there, and local or religious histories should be some help in identifying them.

WM (Wesleyan Methodist)
FRIENDS (Quaker)
EM, ME (Episcopal Methodist)
EL (Evangelical Lutheran)
NC (Methodist New Connexion)

53

MENN (Mennonist, Mennonite)
PM (Primitive Methodist)
C (Congregational or Christian)
BC (Bible Christian)
D, T (Dunkard or Tunker)
CS, KS (Church/Kirk of Scotland
EUB (Evangelical United Brethren)
EU, EV, EA (Evangelical)
UP (United Presbyterian)
RC (Roman Catholic)
FC, FK (Free Church/Kirk)
EP (Episcopalian--Anglican)
CP (Canada Presbyterian)
CE (Church of England--Anglican)
CONG (Congregational)
FW (Free Will Baptist)

DEATHS

Do not neglect to read the column for deaths in 1851 and 1861, part of the personal schedule (deaths during 1851, age and cause; deaths during 1860, age and cause). In 1871 a schedule of deaths was added after the personal schedule, or schedule of the "living" (deaths occuring within the past 12 months, age, birthplace, religion, marital status, and cause of death).

AGRICULTURAL

Also look for agricultural schedules which will give you the property description of the family residence, and an idea of their standard of living (number of animals, farm produce, etc). In **1851** they follow each portion of a township's personal enumeration. In **1861** they are grouped together following all of a county's personal schedules, not necessarily in the same township order as the personal schedules, and often on a different microfilm reel. Be sure you make a note of the "district" or "part" of the township your family appears in. In **1871** there is a separate Schedule 4, for which you must have recorded your family's **line number** from the personal schedule as well as the page number.

1853
AGRICULTURAL

In 1853 a special census was taken by the provincial Department of Agriculture, of some immigrants who had arrived within the past 45-50 years. It is not known how many of these were actually returned, and only 41 have survived. The information tells, among other things, the parish, postal address, county and country from which he emigrated, his occupation there, date of arrival in Canada, age, marital status, and present location. These are stored at PAC (Government Archives Division) from which you can obtain a copy of the individual's return by quoting reference **RG 17 Vol. 2325**. The names are:

CANADIAN FAMILY CENSUS FORM 1852 – 1891

THE McKENZIE FAMILY of PUSLINCH TOWNSHIP

1852 Div. 2 p. 1 — Twp. Puslinch Co. Wellington — C-11743

Names	Occups.	Birthplaces	Religion	Res.	Age	M.S.	Other	House Type/Comments
KENETH	FARM.	SCOT.	F.C.		36	M		
CHRISTIAN		"	"		30	M		
ARCHIBALD		CANADA W.	"		4			
DONALD		"	"		2			
CAMERON, PETER	LAB.	SCOT.	"		60	M		
" MARGARET		"			50	M		

1861 Div. 1 p. 7 — Twp. Ditto Co. — C-1084

Names	Occups.	Birthplaces	Religion	Res.	Age	M.S.	Other	House Type/Comments
KENNETH	FARM.	SCOT.	F.C.		45	M		
MRS.		"	"		35	M		
ARCHY		CANADA	"		13			
DONALD		"	"		11			
ANNIE		"	"		8			
ALEXANDER		"	"		6			
DUNCAN		"	"		4			
KENNETH		"	"		2			
ANN		"	"		15			

1871 Div. 4 p. 15 Line — Twp. Ditto Co. — C-9945

Names	Age	Birthplaces	Religion	Origin	Occupations	M.S.	Other- Comments
KENNETH	57	SCOT.	PRESB.		FARMER	M	
CHRISTENA	48	"	"			M	
ARCHIBALD	22	ONT.	"	SCOTS	FARMER	S	
ANNIE	18	"	"	"		S	
DONALD	20	"	"	"	TEACHER	S	
DUNCAN	14	"	"	"		S	
KENNETH	12	"	"	"		S	
PETER	10	"	"	"		S	
JENET	7	"	"	"		S	
CHRISTENA	5	"	"	"		S	

1881 Div. 1 p. 10 — Twp. Ditto Co. — C-13258

Names	Age	Birthplaces	Religion	Origin	Occupations	M.S.	Other- Comments
CHRISTINA	60	SCOT.	PRESB.		FARMER	W	
ARCHIBALD	31	ONT.	"	SCOTS	"	S	
ANNIE	28	"	"	"		S	
PETER	18	"	"	"		S	AT SCHOOL
CHRISTINA	14	"	"	"		S	" "
CAMPBELL, DONALD	18	"	"	"	SERVANT	S	

1891 Div. 1 p. 19 — Twp. Ditto Co. — T-6377

Names	Age	M.S.	Rela- tion	Self	Birthplaces Father	Mother	Religion	Occupations	Other Comments
ARCHIBALD	41			ONT.	SCOT	SCOT.	PRESB.	FARMER	EMPLOYER
ANNIE	35		SIB.	"	"	"	"		
DUNCAN	33		BRO	"	"	"	"	FARMER	WAGE EARNER
CHRISTENA	23		SIS.	"	"	"	"		
CHRISTENA	69	W	MOTH.	SCOT.	"	"	"		
McCLOUD, KENNETH	53		L	"	"	"	"	WAGE EARNER	

© 1985 Ontario Genealogical Society

Sample of OGS census form

55

Thomas Lamb (Usborne)
Henry Airth (Horton)
John Blake (Goderich)
John Wilson (Guelph)
Robert Cromar (Woolwich)
John Brill (Bagot)
Joseph Barnard (Monaghan)
John Wallon (Bagot)
John Lightfoot (Cavan)
Edward McCrea (Bagot)
Thomas Fee (Emily)
William Filliter (Bagot)
James Sutton (Hamilton, Cavan)
John Windle (Bagot)
Robert Syme (N. Sherbrooke)
Thomas Corrigan (Clarendon)
Samuel Cole (Sarnia)
James Shaw (Clarendon)
William Jenkins (Goderich)
James Rowan (Kincardine)
Henry Rowlings (Plympton)
Charles Robertson (Windham)
Simpson Shepherd (Plympton)
Alexander Smart (Clarendon)
Patrick Kelley (Elizabethtown)
John Breckon (Nelson)
James Wagar (Harwich)
Thomas Alton (Nelson)
Philip VanKoughnet (Cornwall)
Thomas Cairns (Plympton)
Thomas Jowsey (Eardley)
Thomas Earl (Blandford)
John Munro (Horton)
Joseph Matthewson (Blandford)
Donald C. McLean (Eardley)
Joseph Stewart (Elizabethtown)
Walter Beatty (Yonge)
James McQueen (Esquesing, Pilkington)
Ewen McLean (Brock, Kincardine)
Richard Richardson (Goulbourn, Clarendon)
William Hamilton (Ramsay, Clarendon)

CENSUS
FORM
OGS has a comprehensive census form that allows you
to record one family from 1852 to 1891 (illustrated).

5/ Land Records

REFERENCE
DATES

1784	Land grant to Six Nations Indians, Grand River
1788	Four Districts formed (see maps)
1795	Land registry system established in counties
1800	Land grant to Timothy Rogers to establish Quaker settlement in York County
1803	Land grant to Thomas Talbot to establish settlement south of London
1804	Selkirk's Baldoon settlement
1805	German Company settlement, Waterloo County
1815	Beginning of Richmond and Perth settlements, Lanark County; majority of Selkirk settlers leave Red River Colony for Upper Canada
1819	Legislation authorized grants to 1812 War veterans
1823	Peter Robinson emigrants from Ireland began to settle in Lanark and Peterborough Counties
1825	Canada Company incorporated to colonize the Huron Tract and other areas
1847	County registry offices began keeping town and township copybooks of land transactions
1895	Land Titles Act
1901	Grants began for Fenian and South African (Boer) War service
1945	Veterans' Land Act; for military service

Working with land records involves townships, concessions and lots. It was said before that townships remain relatively unchanged since their original surveys. Where Regional government was established in the 1960s, a township may now be part of a certain Regional Municipality, but their boundaries and names are found on older maps, such as Perly's, and are still used by local residents.

CONCESSIONS

Each township was divided into several concessions. Irregularly shaped townships seldom have an easy, neat pattern of concessions. Smaller, detailed maps of townships can be located in a county historical atlas. **BF Concession** refers to a "broken front" -- the result of a natural geographical feature such as a river or lake edge. In researching some townships you will find mysterious mention of initials in a concession reference. This will be a necessary guide to direction of the location. Examples: "NTR" = North of Talbot Road (Norfolk County); "SDR" = South of Durham Road

57

(Bruce County); "EHST" = East of Hurontario Street (Peel County). It may take a little historical research to decipher these meanings so you do not search in the wrong direction for your location.

Gores were sometimes created inadvertently as the irregular result of land between two surveys. Or they may have been a leftover piece of land in a township after being surveyed, not as wide as a regular concession.

GRANT
PROCESS

There were several steps in the land granting process, all of which involved documents in different government departments. Although the regulations of the process changed somewhat every few years, the resulting documents for the ordinary settler can be described as: the initial petition, an Order-in-Council, a warrant to survey, a receipt for fees paid, a fiat authorizing the grant, the Surveyor General's description or location ticket, and the final certificate or patent.

A) Ontario Land Records Index

Prepared by the Archives of Ontario, this most useful index for genealogists, also known as the Computerized Land Records Index, is widely available in genealogical and other major libraries, usually in convenient microfiche form. Any Ontario library with a microfiche reader was given a set. It is the only province-wide index dating from first official settlement. It summarizes original land grants from the Crown, derived from the initial grants, from Canada Company sales and leases, and from grants to Peter Robinson settlers. It does **not** include **subsequent** transactions on any piece of property.

This index can be searched either by surname or by township name. **Always search every spelling variation of your surname**. What it will tell you, whenever the information was available from the original record, is a property description, date and type of grant, and type of transaction. Reference is also made to the original source, which we are told will supply no further information, although rarely there might be a marginal note on a man's residence, helpful only if there is no property description. The index is only a **tool**, and its prime value, beyond that all-important property description, is in leading you to primary sources for additional research.

The columns headed "Date Identity Code", "Transaction Type" and "Type of Free Grant" seem to be overlooked by some searchers (see illustration), and they are the clues to further research.

58

NAME OF LOCATEE	TOWNSHIP / TOWN / CITY	LOT	CONC.	DATE ID.	ISSUE DATE	TRANS TYPE	TYPE FG	TYPE OF LEASE / SALE	ARCHIVAL REFERENCE RG SERIES VOL PG
ELLIOT MATHEW RESIDENCE	MALDEN			8	19970218	FG	OR DEED NO.		01 C13 013 069
ELLIOT MATHEW RESIDENCE				8	17930711 ND	FG	OR DEED NO.		01 C13 014 254
ELLIOT MATTHEW RESIDENCE	PUSLINCH	F1/2 35	9	2	18420305 ND	A	DEED NO.		01 C15 003 200
ELLIOT MATTHEW RESIDENCE	LOGAN	10	5	4	18470605 ND	L	DEED NO.		CC 83 030 375
ELLIOT MATW. RESIDENCE				8	17950620 ND	FG	OR DEED NO.		01 C13 013 068
ELLIOT MICHAEL RESIDENCE	DOURO	E1/2 9	3	1	1826C ND	FG	PR DEED NO.		01 C14 020 031
ELLIOT MOSES RESIDENCE	MARA ELIZABETHTOWN	N1/2 28 & 29	12	8	18170326 ND	FG	SUE DEED NO.		01 C13 081 109
ELLIOT MOSES RESIDENCE	ELIZABETHTOWN ELIZABETHTOWN	E1/2 6	7	2	18340702 ND	FG	COMM DEED NO.		01 C13 091 016
ELLIOT ROBERT RESIDENCE	BURGESS BURGESS	SW 1/2 10	9	8	18211114 ND	FG	ME DEED NO.		01 C13 096 027
ELLIOT ROBERT RESIDENCE	WHITCHURCH WHITCHURCH	15	7	8	18310602 ND	L	CL DEED NO.		01 C13 152 111
ELLIOT ROBERT RESIDENCE	SEYMOUR	SE PT 16	7	1	18330221 ND	S	CL DEED NO.		01 C14 020 221
ELLIOT ROBERT RESIDENCE	PUSLINCH	FT1/2 21	GORE	5	18490224 ND	S	DEED NO.	CL	01 CII13 002 231
ELLIOT ROBT RESIDENCE	SEYMOUR	SE1/2 16	7	5	18330221 ND	S	CL DEED NO.		01 CII13 001 071
ELLIOT ROBT RESIDENCE	ELLICE	24	9	4	18451114 ND	L	DEED NO.		CC 83 030 190
ELLIOT SAMUEL RESIDENCE	ELIZABETHTOWN	1/2 35	2	1	1789C ND	FG	OR DEED NO.		01 AIV 008 103
ELLIOT THOMAS RESIDENCE	EMILY EMILY	NE1/4 7	2	1	18200830 ND	FG	L8 DEED NO.		01 C13 132 144
ELLIOT THOS RESIDENCE	WINGHAM (T)	28 W ARTHUR ST		9	18710224 ND	S	DEED NO.	SCH	01 AIV 002 105

Sample page from the Ontario Land Records Index, alphabetical listing by name of locatee (courtesy Archives of Ontario)

59

DATE IDENTITY	1 (location ticket)	5 (sale)
CODE	2 (assignment)	6 (Canada Company contract)
	3 (patent)	7 (deed)
	4 (lease)	8 (Order-in-Council - "OC")

With further searching, you may be able to find the original or copies of the original of these sources. Most are available at AO. For instance, many of these documents can be found within Township Papers, land petitions, Heir & Devisee Commission records, or Canada Company registers.

CANADA
COMPANY

Canada Company records at AO include such items as contract books, applications for deeds, a register of wills 1826-1920, a register of powers of attorney 1826-1926, and burial certificates 1842-1923. Canada Company **remittance books**, four volumes 1843-52, were kept to record the handling of money through its agents for a specific purpose. The agents were intermediaries in forwarding money from Ontario settlers to relatives and friends overseas, often to assist their emigration. Each volume has a surname index to recipients. The receipt gives the recipient's detailed address in such countries as England, Ireland, Scotland, Germany and France. After the first volume many relationships are specified between sender and recipient. All Canada Company records can be consulted in original form after using the finding aid.

TRANSACTION
TYPE

These are a repeat of four of the above categories. Free grant and assignment are the most important to watch for. **Free grant** indicates that the settler did not pay for the land, so he qualified for this in some way which will appear under the "Type of Free Grant". **Assignment** means that the grant recipient was not the first locatee in the Surveyor General's records. Searching in land petitions, Township Papers, and Heir & Devisee records may give more information. Normally it is much more difficult to find information on a person who appears as "leasing" land. You may be able to go on and find a petition for him, or you may find something in Township Papers, but if he never became a **landowner** you will likely find little evidence of him in land records. This is particularly true when you investigate deeds, as many leases and rental of properties were informal and unregistered agreements.

| FG (free grant) | S (sale) |
| L (lease) | A (assignment) |

TYPE OF
FREE GRANT

These supply the most detailed clues, if your ancestor fell into this category. There were many regulations or qualifying factors for a free grant, and they changed from time to time. Different categories of free land grants were those who paid full fees (see below), reduced fees, or no fees. After 1826, free grants were discontinued to all but Loyalist and military or militia claimants, and later immigrants had to purchase land from the Crown or some other source.

OR (Old Regulations)	ME (Military Emigrant)
NR (New Regulations)	LB (Land Board)
FF (Full Fees)	PR (Peter Robinson settler)
UE (Loyalist)	SE (Scotch Emigrant)
DUE (Daughter of Loyalist)	AA (Gratuitous or Hardship grant)
SUE (Son of Loyalist)	1819 (Regulations)
MC (Military Claimant)	1820 (Regulations)
COMM (Heir & Devisee)	1825 (Regulations)
M (Militia)	V (Veteran - Fenian, South African War)

In this list, most designations can lead the genealogist to other records sources. For the three types of **Loyalist** grants see Chapter 11. A free grant generally meant not paying for the land, but certain administrative fees (**Full Fees**) were required. Loyalists did not have to pay these fees. **Military Claimants** (disbanded or pensioned soldiers of the British Army) did, and so did other settlers. **Military Emigrant** refers to settlers who arrived here for the Perth and Richmond settlements in Lanark County, and who were initially administered by the Quarter Master General's Department of the British Army. Grants were made to sons (**Scotch Emigrants**) of some of these new arrivals, only for one year, as an incentive to emigrate.

Heir & Devisee Commission records are discussed later in this Chapter. **Militia** grants were made in two phases: from 1816-17 to strategically distribute ex-soldiers for possible defense purposes; from 1819-20 to veterans of the militia who took part in the War of 1812. **Veterans'** grants from 1901 were also an award for service either during the Fenian uprisings in the 1860s or in the South African War. **Land Board** refers to certificates issued by the four original District Land Boards for a five-year period, 1789-94. **Gratuitous** grants were made to certain indigent settlers after government review who barely subsisted and could not afford the fees, which were then waived.

In *Families*, Vol. 14, No. 4 (1975), John Mezaks, has an article called "Crown Grants in the Home District: The System and the Existing Records". Although written for a seminar on the Home District, the article covers the system of land regulations for all of Upper Canada. See also Patricia Kennedy's article "Records of the Land Granting Process: Pre-Confederation", in *Families*, Vol. 16, No. 4 (1977) or Gates' *Land Policies of Upper Canada* for understanding the intricacies of types of grants.

More detailed description of the OLRI can be found in my article "An Interpretation of the Ontario Land Records Index" in *Families*, Vol. 25, No. 2 (1986). For early families in the Lanark County area, see "Military Land Granting in Upper Canada Following the War of 1812" by Eric Jarvis, in *Ontario History*, Vol. LXVII.

CROWN
LANDS

AO has a finding aid called *Preliminary Inventory of the Records of the Surveyor-General, 1763-1845, Crown Lands Department, 1827-1905, Department of Lands and Forests, 1906-1972, Ministry of Natural Resources, 1972- (RG 1)*, with several appendices. We will call this the "Crown Lands finding aid".

B) Upper Canada Land Petitions

A petition to the Lieutenant Governor in Council was the beginning of the process to acquire a piece of Crown land before 1827. These are mainly in the free grant category. PAC holds the original Upper Canada Land Petitions; both PAC and AO have microfilm copies. A person might have petitioned shortly after arrival here while temporarily living in a town or with relatives, or he might have found a suitable piece of land and began to settle immediately, applying later for the grant.

Some petitions are very straightforward and give little information about the petitioner, other than his presence in the province at that date. Others may give their arrival date in Canada, their birthplace, marital status, number in family, or any eligibility for a special type of free grant. When sons and daughters of Loyalists petitioned for their free land grants, they gave their father's name to support their claims. Many times oaths of allegiance to the Crown or affidavits from character witnesses are included with petitions.

INDEX

The petitions are indexed by surname and this is another case where you should search all variant spellings. One family was stymied for years because they failed to find petitions for all the sons and daughters of a Loyalist named See. It was discovered that the surname See had been mis-read because of the old handwriting and had been indexed as "Lee" for about half the petitions.

A name, place, date and reference number are on the index. The placename is not necessarily where the set-

Sample of Upper Canada Land Petition, RG 1, L3, F Bundle 12/58, (courtesy Archives of Ontario) tler lived or planned to live. He may have been applying from the nearest town, or through a land agent in a large town, and that place name might have ended up on the index cards.

PROPERTY
DESCRIPTION

You will seldom find property descriptions in a petition itself, unless the petitioner was already on the property and asking for a patent to it. However, if a petition was "recommended" by the Executive Council, its date can often be connected with an entry and location on the OLRI.

LAND BOOKS

On the index to petitions are also references to Land Books which record their receipt in Executive Council minutes. Searching the actual book will add next to no information other than names of other petitioners recorded the same day. However, if an original petition has not survived, the Land Book entry will at least be a reference point. Useful reading: "Deciphering the Upper Canada Land Books and Land Petitions" by Patricia Kennedy in *Readings in Ontario Genealogical Sources.*

Men petitioning for **military** or **militia** claims will state the name of their regiment or company with dates of service. Some supplementary documents were filed with these for proof, such as a commanding officer's statement or a statement of service, but not all are extant and/or microfilmed. Where service in the British Army was involved, this is a perfect lead to British War Office records in the Public Record Office in London (and on LDS microfilm), or possibly to the Military "C" Series at PAC and AO (see Chapter 10).

OTHER
PETITIONS

While Upper Canada Land Petitions are still the most consulted group, there are other series of petitions at AO. These are found through the Crown Lands finding aid, its Appendix I, and include petitions to the Commissioner of Crown Lands post-1826, petitions extracted from Township Papers during the microfilming of that series, and petitions and accompanying papers for grants 1901-22 for service in the Fenian raids and South African War.

C) Orders-in-Council, Fiats, Warrants

These are documents that were issued by the government or Executive Council, as it was called, as part of the granting process. Originals and microfilmed copies are at AO. Again, the Crown Lands finding aid, Appendix I, shows you how to find them. When a land petition is missing, these documents provide primary

FORM F.

AFFIDAVIT OF COMRADE.

(FENIAN RAID.)

I, *Daniel Holliday*, of the *Township*
of *Whitby* in the *County* of *Ontario*,
having myself served in the active militia of Canada in the defence of the frontier of the Province of
Ontario, in the year *1866*, make oath and say as follows:—

1. That *James Stocks*, whose affidavit appears above, was to my
certain knowledge enrolled in the Volunteer Militia of Canada in Ontario in the year *1862*, and
performed active service at the time and place set forth in his affidavit.

2. That to the best of my knowledge and belief the facts set forth in his said affidavit are true
and correct.

Sworn before me at *Township*
of Whitby
in the *County of Ontario*

this *16* day of *Aug* 19*07*.

D Holliday

Beall J. P.

To be forwarded to the senior surviving officer of the corps to which applicant belonged.

I, *John E Farewell Lt Col comy 34th Regt* hereby certify that the within named
James Stocks served as *a private*
in the *Ontario Columbus Rifles* in the defence of the frontier of this Province
in the year *1866*, and to the best of my knowledge the facts set forth in the above affidavits are
true and correct *As I subsequently commanded said company am
aware of the facts stated* (Name) *John E Farewell*
(Rank) *Lt Col*
(Corps) *34th Regiment*

Dated at *Whitby*

this *24th* day of *August*
19*01*
To be returned to
THE COMMISSIONER OF CROWN LANDS,
TORONTO.

Affidavit from petition for land grant, Fenian Raid service, RG 1, C-VII-2,
#18779/01 (courtesy Archives of Ontario)

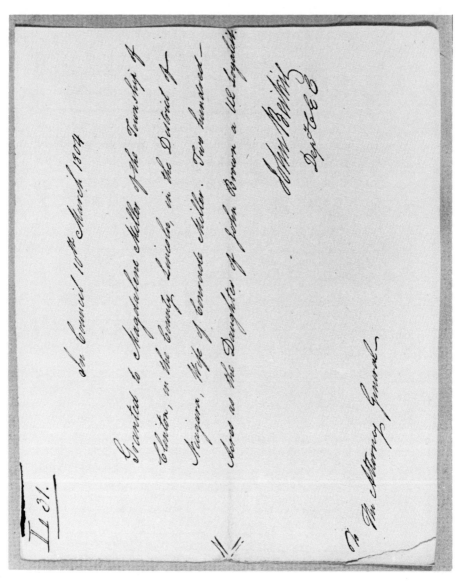

A Fiat issued in 1804, RG 1, C-I-3 (courtesy Archives of Ontario)

evidence of a person's involvement in the process, with a date and place (see illustration).

D) Patents

A patent was eventually issued to an individual who successfully obtained a grant of Crown land, after the administrative procedures and the fulfillment of certain settlement duties if it was not a free grant. The latter could include clearing a portion of land, erecting buildings, completing payments, and performing statutory labour in the community.

Although **certificates** for land were issued by District Land Boards from 1783, it was not until 1795 that actual patents were issued. In that twelve-year period various other documents were used as temporary substitutes, as mentioned in the OLRI section. Settlers were called "squatters" until they were able to undertake the process. Sometimes patents were not issued until years after the process began, for want of money to make payments, or problems with performing settlement duties.

INDEXES, COPIES

Patents have been indexed by **surname** 1795-1825 and by **township** up to 1850, and they are on microfilm at AO. Complete indexes up to the present day are located at the Ontario Ministry of Natural Resources, Official Documents Section. The patents themselves are stored at the Official Documents Section, Ministry of Government Services, from which you can obtain a copy by giving them the name of owner, property description and date of patent. (Appendix I)

E) Heir and Devisee Commission

Records of the first Commission 1797-1804 are at PAC, but copies are expected at AO. Records of the second Commission 1805-1911 are at AO. The job of the Commission was to clarify land titles where patents had not yet been issued. There were several reasons that could cause a claim to be made. When the original nominee for a Crown land grant had died or left the property, an heir, devisee or assignee had to apply to the Commission with proof of his right to the patent. For instance, if a man died without a will or transference of title, his eldest son could apply for the claim at age 21.

DOCUMENTS

Some of the supporting documents given in evidence might include old land certificates, location tickets, copies of wills, mortgages, receipts, affidavits, assignments or letters. They are a real treasure for a genealogist because of their attempt to establish relationships. A patent would be issued to the claimant if the Commission accepted the evidence and if the Sur-

PROVINCE OF CANADA.

VICTORIA, *by the Grace of God, of the United Kingdom of Great Britain and Ireland, QUEEN, Defender of the Faith.*

To all to whom these Presents shall come—Greeting:

Whereas *Kenneth MacKenzie of the Township of Puslinch in the County of Wellington, yeoman*

with Our Commissioner for the sale of Our Crown Lands, duly authorized by Us in this behalf, for the absolute purchase, at and for the price and sum of *Eighty one pounds five Shillings* hath contracted and agreed to and of lawful money of Our said Province, of the Lands and Tenements hereinafter mentioned and described, of which We are seized in right of Our Crown. NOW KNOW YE, that in consideration of the said sum of *Eighty one pounds five Shillings* by *him* the said *Kenneth MacKenzie* to Our said Commissioner of Crown Lands, in hand well and truly paid to Our use, at or before the sealing of these Our Letters Patent, We have granted, sold, aliened, conveyed and assured, and by these Presents do grant, sell, alien, convey and assure, unto the said *Kenneth Mac Kenzie his* Heirs and Assigns for ever, All that Parcel or Tract of Land, situate, lying and being in the Town *ship* of *Puslinch* in the County of *Wellington.* of Our said Province, containing by admeasurement *one hundred acres* be the same more or less ; which said Parcel or Tract of Land may be otherwise known as follows, that is to say : being composed of

The Rear or North East half of the late Clergy Reserve Lot number Seventeen in the Tenth Concession of the aforesaid Township of Puslinch

Recorded 21st Jany 1856

Dept Reg

To have and to hold the said Parcel or Tract of Land hereby granted, conveyed and assured, unto the said *Kenneth Mac Kenzie his* heirs and assigns for ever; saving, excepting and reserving, nevertheless unto Us, Our Heirs and Successors, all Mines of Gold and Silver, and the free use, passage and enjoyment of, in, over and upon all navigable waters that shall or may be hereafter found on or under, or be flowing through or upon any part of the said Parcel or Tract of Land hereby granted as aforesaid.

GIVEN under the Great Seal of Our Province of Canada: Witness, Our Trusty and Well-beloved SIR EDMUND WALKER HEAD, Baronet, Governor General of British North America, and Captain General and Governor in Chief in and over Our Provinces of Canada, Nova Scotia, New Brunswick, and the Island of Prince Edward, and Vice-Admiral of the same, &c., &c., &c. At TORONTO, this *Seventh* day of *January* in the year of Our Lord, one thousand eight hundred and fifty-six, and in the *nineteenth* year of Our Reign.

By Command of His Excellency in Council.

Geo. Et Cartier
Secretary.

Commissioner of Crown Lands.

A land patent dated 1856 (Official Documents Section, Ontario Ministry of Government Services, see Appendix I)

veyor General's Office (up to 1827) or Crown Lands Office (after 1827) approved the validity of the original nominee's title.

These records are indexed alphabetically by surname of claimant. More details can be found in "Records of the Heir and Devisee Commission", *Families*, Vol. 16, No. 4 (1977) by John Mezaks. Another useful article is "The Family Compact at Work: The Second Heir and Devisee Commission of Upper Canada, 1805-1841" by H. Pearson Gundy in *Ontario History*, Vol. 66, No. 3 (1974).

F) Township Papers

This group of records is arranged by township, concession and lot number, so knowing the property description is essential to using them. These are papers referring to a specific lot and might contain a variety of documents or letters about claims to the property, and transfers of a claim, prior to the patent.

Here you can find evidence of a man's occupation of property in a time period when census and other records are usually not available. Sometimes you may find material relating to neighbours' squabbles over fence lines, inadequate surveys, or complaints from non-resident owners about squatters. If a man left Ontario before receiving a patent, this series might be one of your few sources of information. Documents do not exist for every property, but there are cross-references to other locations if a man owned more than one.

The Crown Lands finding aid, Appendix H, is your guide.

G) Abstract Indexes to Deeds

Subsequent land transactions, after the original patent, were and are registered at County Land Registry Offices, and can be found by using the Abstract Index. Copies for all southern Ontario townships are on microfilm at AO up to about 1858. Northern Ontario districts are **not** microfilmed at AO, so for them and for all **original** Abstract books, the local Office must be visited. In general they keep "regular" office hours and are often crowded with members of the real estate and legal professions. Both search and copying fees are charged.

Again, you must know the exact property description to search Abstract books, as they are arranged by concession and lot within each township. In the case of a village, town or city, they can be found by subdivision

District of Wellington
To Wit

3115

Personally appeared before
Me Wm Leslie Esqr One of Her Majesties Justices
of the Peace for the District aforesaid John Black
and William McKenzie both of the Township of
Puslinch and Maketh Oath that to the Best
of their Knowledge North half of Lot 17. Tenth
Concession of Puslinch has been occupied since
the Spring fall of Eighteen Hundred and Forty one
and that they are Personally acquainted with
~~Wm Williams~~ present Occupier of said
Lot that he has a House and a Barn and about
Thirty acres cleared on said lot all which is true

Sworn before me at Puslinch
this 4th day of January 1847

Worship J.P.

John Black
William McKenzie

acknowledges 7 years
&c

Sample document from Township Papers (Puslinch), RG 1, C-IV (courtesy Archives of Ontario) plan or street location. Since 1895 the Land Titles Office certifies titles in the northern districts of the province, and some southern counties.

Subdivision of an original 100 acre lot into small lots for a village or town creates problems in trying to follow ownership. At some point a plan of subdivision will take over from the original property description. It is very important to make notes of all references to plan numbers or names, and continuation of pages.

INSTRUMENTS

From this abstract you will learn when an ancestor's name first appeared, the type of instrument or document (deed, bargain and sale -- "B & S", mortgage, quit claim, etc.), date of instrument, date of registry, instrument number, grantee and grantor. **Grantor** is the person making the grant or mortgaging the property; **grantee** is the person receiving the grant or to whom the property is mortgaged. Use the instrument number and date to look at or copy the original document in a Registry Office.

Following the ancestral name in the abstract tells purchase date and indicates his sale date or possible death on that property.

UNPROBATED
WILLS

Wills may be shown in the abstract as registered land documents. This is an important source for unprobated wills that were used to transfer or convey property. The instrument number of a will in this case refers, like the other documents, to the Registry Office number, not to Surrogate Court records. After 1865, wills which do not specify a property description are recorded in the General Register series of each Registry Office (see below).

H) Deeds

All deeds or instruments were registered at one of these Land Registry Offices. You can obtain copies for a nominal fee by quoting its number, township and date. "Deeds" on microfilm at AO up to about 1876 are actually **copybooks** of deeds. A copy cannot be made from the microfilm because originals are not in AO custody. A copy for your own use can be obtained from the original document at the appropriate Registry Office, or from an original copybook at its current location.

Most documents will at least establish a date and place for your ancestor. Even from the early 1800s a wife was often named on a sale to bar her dower right, which helps to identify a family. Occasionally other family relationships are mentioned, or a woman conveying land as "widow of" so-and-so. If you do not find the

71

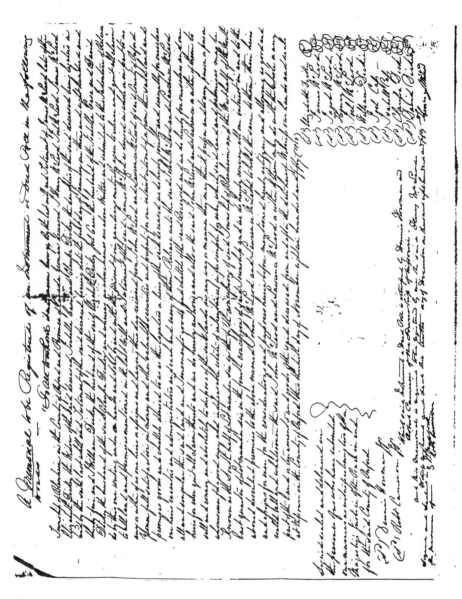

Sample of a copybook deed referring to a will of 1835 with list of heirs, Blenheim township 1850, Deed #2813 (courtesy Woodstock Public Library)

name you seek in any transactions, the man likely only rented the property. This might be confirmed by assessment or collectors' rolls, the agricultural schedule of a census, or a local directory near the date in question.

Always check the date of the instrument and the date of its registry. Several years' discrepancy might indicate some family event, such as death of a grantee or removal of the family to other parts, immediately before registration of the instrument.

COPYBOOKS

From 1797 when the land registration system was set up, until 1847, the exchange of property was not only entered in the Abstract Index, but was also registered as **memorials** in county copybooks, or memorial books. The memorial did not necessarily contain the full text of the original document, and for early days there is some doubt now as to where originals were kept. It may be that the concerned parties kept them. From 1865 on, county clerks discontinued "memorializing" and copied the full text of documents.

Copybooks are useful when original documents are missing or have not been microfilmed. In 1955 copybooks were discontinued entirely.

When you find a reference number to an instrument predating 1847, you can see the memorial by consulting the microfilmed **county** copybook at AO. From 1847 a change in the system produced copybooks of memorials recorded by **townships**. Some, not all, county copybooks are indexed by surnames. If you know only the county where your ancestor lived without an exact property description, you may have to search every page of a copybook to find his transactions and what properties they related to.

Sometimes you can search the index to township copybooks and find references to deeds earlier than 1847, although it's difficult to determine since few indexes include dates. If you are working with the pre-1847 period and are having little luck, the relevant township deeds index might help. Certainly in the case of indexes to some townships in Prince Edward County there are references to deeds much earlier than 1847, and to find them you must then consult the county, not the township, copybook.

The old county copybooks were given to AO custody, and they have now been distributed to regional libraries throughout the province. Locations for them are listed in McFall's *Land Records in Ontario Registry Offices*.

To that list, we amend that York County copybooks are now at the University of Waterloo.

A word of caution here about using the microfilmed copybooks at AO. These were filmed some years ago by the Genealogical Society of Utah, now catalogued in AO's "GS" series. Be sure to check the description of an entry on the card catalogue with the description on the box containing the microfilm. Then compare both with the contents of the microfilm itself. The name or contents of the book, volume number and dates covered may not be correct.

In addition, some books or indexes may not have been available at that time for microfilming. Some books may not have survived at all which causes great frustration for the searcher with a reference number and no reference. This is a confusing area for the experienced as well as the novice researcher. Try to work methodically, don't take anything for granted, and know precisely what source you are using.

GENERAL REGISTERS

There are also **General Registers**, a copybook series from 1866 for each county which includes such land-related documents as wills, bankruptcies and powers of attorney. They are indexed by names. Not every county is represented in this microfilmed collection at AO.

Some other functions of Registry Offices over the years have been the recording of naturalizations (see Chapter 7), railway debentures and court judgments. Their vaults also sometimes became repositories for local municipal, police, school boards, and other companies or institutions that may have lacked security storage. Any such material that is discovered is being or will be distributed to regional or local resource centres with an obvious interest. Papers or collections of a private rather than government nature will be eventually catalogued at AO.

ADDRESSES

OGS has for sale the above mentioned booklet called *Land Records in Ontario Registry Offices* by David and Jean McFall, which goes into more detail about the land registration system. Also included is "The History of the Land Record Copy Books" by Shirley Spragge, an explanation of that series. Addresses are given for every Registry and Land Titles Office, along with the list of repositories now holding the copybooks.

6/ Court Records

REFERENCE
DATES

1793	Establishment of provincial Probate Court and district Surrogate Courts
1827	Probate and Surrogate Court jurisdiction extended to guardianships
1842	District Councils replace Courts of General Quarter Sessions
1850	Surrogate Courts became county rather than district jurisdictions
1858	Probate Court was abolished
1884	Married Women's Property Act; married women allowed disposal of property and earnings, e.g. through wills
1914	Succession Duty Act terms applied to all estates; inventories and lists of heirs were recorded

The Ontario Archives is the custodian of estate records for the province. Until 1793, **Prerogative Courts** dealt with estate matters. Almost nothing has survived from this period with the exception of some records for the former Hesse (Western) District and Luneburg (Eastern) District. Four early files exist in the Leeds and Grenville court, and one for the Western District in Essex court. The total of 24 names are listed in Catherine Shepard's book *Surrogate Court Records at the Archives of Ontario.*

From 1793 to 1858 the two courts involved in probate and administration of estates were the Surrogate Court and the Probate Court. The AO finding aid *Preliminary Inventory of Court Records, RG 22* (we will call it Court records finding aid) is the guide to using all Surrogate records from 1793 up to twenty years ago.

A) Probate Court

PROBATE

The Probate Court had jurisdiction over estates involving property valued at L5 or more, and in more than one district. In 1858 this "central" court was abolished and the Surrogate Courts became the only court dealing with deceased's estates, with jurisdiction by county of the property involved.

Probate Court records are at AO with a surname index (Appendix F of the Court records finding aid) and this has been published by OGS as *Court of Probate: Registers and Estate Files at the Archives of Ontario (1793-1859).* The index gives the name of deceased, his residence, date of will and occupation or status. The actual files may not show date of death. You can infer that death occurred between the date of the will and the date of the probate.

B) Surrogate Court

The Surrogate Court was first responsible for estates with property in one district only, while the Probate Court existed. The system for filing and keeping these records varied from place to place, which explains how much or how little material you may find. Surviving pre-1858 files are now located with a county which was part of an original district. For instance, Niagara District files are with Lincoln County, and Gore District with Wentworth County.

AO now has a comprehensive **surname index** to all Surrogate Court records 1793-1858 (Appendix H of the Court records finding aid), another invaluable tool for genealogists. This quickly leads you to the appropriate card entry for microfilm. Abstracts from early **Kingston** and vicinity wills 1790-1858 have been published, as have **London** District wills 1800-1839 (see Appendix II).

Surname indexes for counties began in 1858 when the Surrogate Court took over sole responsibility for probate and administration. County indexes vary in content; some may only give a name and number, while some may include the year or residence. Many will show two or three reference numbers, such as grant number, non-contentious business (NCB) number, and/or registry book number. You need to make an exact note of all numbers since there was no uniform indexing method for all counties. Either Shepard's *Surrogate Court Records at the Archives of Ontario*, published by OGS, or the Court records finding aid at AO will tell which number of several is the right one to locate the estate file in a particular county. Occasionally it is necessary to consult a register book first, if it is the only reference number, in order to find the estate file number.

Indexes on microfilm at AO generally extend to the 1960s, often in a consecutive series. It can be helpful to know that occasionally a county decided to be especially efficient, and alphabeticized an index by the first vowels after each surname initial. For example, under "B", you would find "Baker", "Beaton", "Blight", "Brougham", and "Bundy" in separate indexes. If you are looking for "Blight" and you search only the first "Ba" index without realizing that there is more, you could end up baffled. Some instances where this occurs is in Waterloo County's first index and York County's second index. New indexes by June Gibson to post 1858 Surrogate Court files are being published serially in *Canadian Genealogist*. These are extracted from the actual microfilmed files rather than from the old indexes. Once in a while a file is missing from the microfilm, and this compiler has then checked to see if the original is available at AO. Also included on these indexes are "fugitive" files (those not appearing in register books) and guardianships. The indexes are available at AO in manuscript form. Generation Press, publisher of *Canadian Genealogist*, has issued the index for Norfolk County as a separate publication.

ESTATE FILES

Your prime concern is with the "grant" of probate, or estate file, which contains the **original** documents. Estate files up to twenty years past are in AO custody. They have been microfilmed to 1900. In addition, York County Surrogate files from 1920 to 1945 have also been microfilmed. Original files from 1900 to twenty years past are available upon retrieval from an off-site storage centre, which takes a few days. The Court records finding aid will give you the correct series number for retrieval, and you must add name of county court, name of deceased, and file reference number.

For more current files within the last twenty years, and for Surrogate indexes after the 1960s, the local county courthouse must be visited. Probate files are in the public domain and there is no problem with access or copying, except maybe having to wait in a line-up.

LETTERS OF ADMINISTRATION

Material found in the files might include a **will** or **letters of administration**. The latter, which result when the deceased was intestate, does not usually have as much information as a will. However, many administrations do include releases from children of deceased (and their residences) in favour of the administrator, be he a local relative, creditor or solicitor. You will learn date and place of death, occupation and property description(s) if applicable. The name of the applicant for administering the estate appears of course; often this is the widow or a child, with the relationship specified.

Administration **with will annexed** usually results from a will that has not appointed executors. Administration **de bonis non** involves some change in the executorship originally appointed in the will. The appointed executor may have died in the meantime or renounced his responsibility in favour of another. The will itself is still primary evidence in the file.

WILLS

Almost everyone is familiar with the general form of a will. If a spouse is not mentioned, it's likely that he or she predeceased the testator. Wills and estate files for married women before 1884 are a good indication that their husbands died first, and they will be described as "widow of the late so-and-so". **Not all children are necessarily named in a will.** Older children may have received "benefits" before the will was made; estrangements could have caused others to be deliberately omitted.

A bonus in a will is reference to married daughters or to grandchildrens' full names or other relatives. Ambiguous terminology might have been used in the early nineteenth century, like "daughter" for daughter-in-law or "nephew" for a sibling's or a cousin's child. You might find an executor or a witness with the same surname as the deceased who is not mentioned in the text of the will but who possibly is a relative of the testator.

Codicils to a will take place when the testator has changed his mind about the distribution of his estate. At times they may follow the maturing, death or estrangment of a child, or reflect a changed circumstance in the estate.

Remember that court records are not the only source for locating a will. In Chapter 5, Sections G and H, this book mentioned unprobated wills found among land records like deeds and general registers. It has been estimated by some researchers that as many as 50% of existing wills were not probated through a court. Wills are also found among Heir and Devisee Commission papers and Canada Company records.

INVENTORIES

Pre-1840s inventories were very detailed, but were not included or microfilmed with each and every estate. Household goods, farm stock and equipment, real estate, insurance and promissory notes were part of them. Later, if available, inventories contained less details of personal property. From 1914 every estate was required by the Succession Duty Act to show property owned and a list of heirs with their addresses. If some children or relatives were not named in the will, then they will not appear on this schedule.

An interesting article for background study is "Wills and Inventories: Records of Life and Death in a Developing Society" by Brian Osborne in *Families*, Vol. 19, No. 4 (1980). Shepard's *Surrogate Court Records at the Archives of Ontario* is extremely useful for background and for its three appendices on pre-1793 estate files, current holdings at AO, and method of indexing for each county.

Not finding a will or administration for an ancestor in the county where he is known to have died, implies that he was not a property owner and/or did not have sufficient personal estate to warrant his family undertaking the expense of legal process.

REGISTERS

Registers are copybooks made by the Surrogate Court Registrar of grants of probate and letters of administration. A copy of the will, or petition for administration will be included. Remember that these books are **copies**, and it is always advisable to consult the original documents whenever possible. A few estate files have been lost or misplaced over the years, and this is when the registers prove of most value.

GUARDIANSHIP

Guardianship papers are a good source of family information, but official occurrences were not common before 1858. Since 1827, guardianship cases were included in Surrogate Court records and their indexes. These could tell you name of deceased parent, names and ages of children, and name of applicant for guardianship, who was often a relative. **Minor** or **infant** children were under 21 years of age.

It was rare for a father to apply for guardianship when his wife died, as he was considered to "own" the children. You will find that it was usually the widow or male relative of the deceased father who applied.

C) Surrogate Clerk's Application Books

With the establishment of the county Surrogate Court system, a central register was kept from 1859 of every application received in the province, whether for probate or administration. This system is a real boon for genealogists in that the surname index covers the whole province, a great asset when place and date of death are unknown.

INDEX

The index up to 1967 is on microfilm at AO, and original index books are available there from 1968 to 1976. From 1977 to the present day, indexes and application books must be consulted at the Surrogate Clerk's Office (Appendix I). The index directs you to the chronological application books, by using the reference number of deceased and the **year** of occurrence.

APPLICATION
BOOKS

You select the application book that contains the year you are looking for, and consult the numbered entry. Here you find name of deceased, residence at death,

79

To Samuel Bealey Harrison Esquire
Surrogate for the Home District of the
Province of Canada

The Petition of Moses Spencer of the Township
of Etobicoke in the Home District Yeoman Humbly
Sheweth

That Conrad Kake late of the Township of
Etobicoke aforesaid Yeoman, deceased departed this
life on or about the Seventh day of November in
the year of our Lord one thousand eight hundred and
Forty, Intestate, leaving Elizabeth Kake his Widow
and four children vg: Jonas Ky, Sidney, Esther ann, Elizabeth and albert
him surviving.

That since the decease of the said Conrad Kake
Your petitioner married the said Elizabeth Kake, who is
still living.

That it is the wish of the said Elizabeth Kake
now the wife of your petitioner, that your petitioner
should be appointed Guardian of the said children
Kake during their minorities

Your Petitioner therefore prays that
Your Honourable Court will be pleased to appoint
him Guardian of the said children during their
minorities on his giving the security required by law.

And your petitioner will ever pray

Toronto Dec 6th 1848.

Moses Spencer

Petition for guardianship, 1848, York County Surrogate Court, RG 22, Series 305
(courtesy Archives of Ontario)

date of death and probate, and name, occupation and residence of applicant (executor or administrator). The **county** in which probate or administration was granted, leads you to the next step -- searching the county Surrogate index to find the estate file, as discussed above.

D) General Quarter Sessions of the Peace (AO)

QUARTER
SESSIONS

Local District Courts of General Quarter Sessions of the Peace provided, in effect, local government up to 1841. Surviving records are accessible at AO with assistance from either the Municipal records finding aid, or the following appendices of the Court records finding aid:

A - Brockville (Johnstown District) 1798-1845
B - Cobourg (Newcastle District) 1805-46
C - Cornwall (Eastern District) 1815-50
D - Cobourg (Newcastle District) 1802-46
E - Brockville (Johnstown District) 1801-19
I - Cobourg (roads and bridges reports) 1810-41
L - Western District (roads and bridges reports) 1821-46

Names of district officials appear here, along with anyone who became involved with administration of daily life or "disturbing the peace". For example, one would apply to the court for a licence to operate a tavern or to perform marriages. There are roads reports, lands sold for tax arrears, registers of fines, releases of dower rights and lists of jurors. The court heard and judged cases of theft, forgery, fraud, arson, profanity, larceny, assault, rape, murder, and all manner of law-breaking.

The minute books of many courts have survived, which are really the key material. Besides possibly finding an ancestor's name and establishing his residence at the time, you will see some social background to the period. Minutes for the **Home District** 1800-11 and for the **London District** 1800-09, 1813-18 were published in the 21st and 22nd (respectively) *Reports of the Department of Public Records and Archives of Ontario* (1932 and 1933).

E) Other Court Records (AO)

Other court records are held at AO -- Chancery Court, Common Pleas, Error and Appeal, Courts of Requests, King's Bench, Assizes, etc., and may only be of interest to the occasional genealogist who finds a reference in some other source. With the exception of criminal or Chancery actions, few will be of much genealogical value. Court records can be a veritable maze to most of us, since their evolution has caused so many changes in name and jurisdiction. And not all series of records may be catalogued or readily accessible.

Judgment docketbooks from Court of King's Bench 1796-1849 tell names of plaintiffs and defendants, occupations and residences, district of the action, details and date of the judgment. However few dockets or transcripts are available.

Many court proceedings began at a local or county level, continuing to a higher court, and generating mountains of paperwork over the years. Tons of paper have been destroyed in the past through fire, flood or lack of storage space at a courthouse. The Court records finding aid and possibly consultation with a specific AO archivist will be a must for any who want to pursue an esoteric legal reference

INQUESTS

Coroners' Inquests are often sought for genealogical information, but not a great amount is available. At AO the *Preliminary Inventory of the Records of the Ministry of the Solicitor General* lists some early records 1800-23. This particular ministry did not exist between 1867 and 1972. Later records include Forensic Science and Pathology files (Appendix 8 of the inventory) 1931-51, indexed alphabetically by surname. These were specific reports sent to the Chief Coroner and do not represent all inquests of the period.

The Chief Coroner's inquest files 1949-80 deal with highly visible or publicized tragedies, for example victims of the *Noronic* ship fire in Toronto harbour in 1949. Although access restrictions are not noted in the finding aid, it is probably safe to say that a 30-50 year policy will apply.

The existence of inquest reports made by county coroners vary in number and time periods. They are not catalogued so this is a one of those circumstances where a knowledgeable archivist might be able to help.

CRIMINAL

"Criminal" trials, as opposed to "civil" trials can be found in minute books of the **Court of Oyer and Terminer and General Gaol Delivery** or trial papers of the later **Assize Courts**. At AO, the most accessible records are **Supreme Court Judges' Benchbooks,** Appendix K of the Court records finding aid. These records cover a wide range of Chief Justices from 1827 to 1885. Also, criminal and civil files 1871-1955 are indexed chronologically with names, case details and reference numbers in several appendices to the *Preliminary Inventory of the Records of the Attorney General*, where restrictions to access do not apply after 50 years.

Police, jail and prison records will be addressed in Chapter 12.

CHANCERY

Chancery Court from 1837 dealt with matters of **equity**, as in estates of minors or "lunatics", foreclosure of mortgages, trusts, partnership settlements and other business of a personal nature. There is as yet no inventory or finding aid at AO for this large collection, and the appropriate archivist must be consulted. The finding of a Chancery Court reference often comes through the search of a property's Abstract index. Judgments affecting a piece of property were registered at a Land Registry Office, but obtaining a copy of the registered document may not yield much information.

NEWSPAPER
REPORTS

Local newspapers always carried details of court proceedings. Even"minor" offenses are usually reported, providing insight to an ancestor that no other source could. Their colourful coverage of the more lurid and tragic events can add contemporary flavour to a family history. Since so few inquest records have survived, newspapers, when available, may be an excellent alternative source of death and family information.

TREASON

Prosecution of traitors to the Crown occurred most notably after the War of 1812 and the 1837 Rebellion. Records of such proceedings were kept according to the government agency involved. **Court of King's Bench** should be investigated in the finding aid. At AO and PAC the Calendar to **Upper Canada Sundries** can lead into the Civil Secretary's correspondence and information about trials for treason in 1838. A **High Treason Register** was compiled many years ago (PAC and AO),listing names alphabetically for the 1812-14 period, with extra information on some, not all, names. An index to this has been published by Brant Branch OGS.

Not all traitors and rebels were summarily hanged; many disappeared quickly without being captured, leaving behind only witnesses' affidavits attesting to treason. After the Rebellion of 1837, 92 rebels were sent to Tasmania for life; some were transported for shorter periods or banished from Ontario for life. Pardons were sometimes issued later on. Lesser transgressors, by far the majority of rebels, were pardoned on security of good behaviour. Upper Canada Sundries contain details of these hearings, including dates and places of transgressions, and are arranged chronologically.

DIVORCE

Divorce is both a court function in the eyes of the law and a "vital statistic" for genealogists, as covered in Chapter 2.

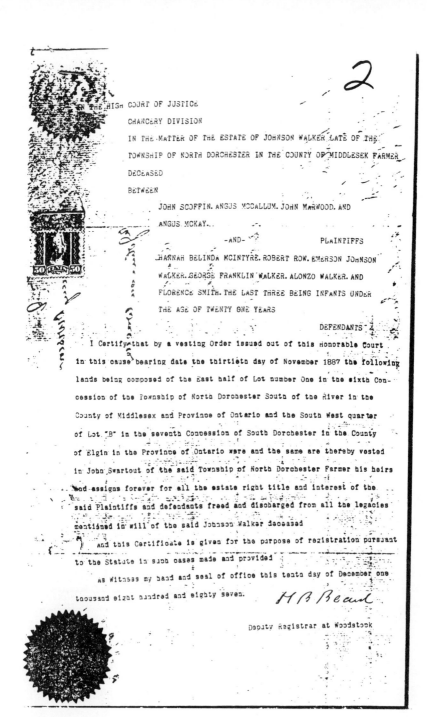

IN THE HIGH COURT OF JUSTICE

CHANCERY DIVISION

IN THE MATTER OF THE ESTATE OF JOHNSON WALKER LATE OF THE

TOWNSHIP OF NORTH DORCHESTER IN THE COUNTY OF MIDDLESEX FARMER

DECEASED

BETWEEN

JOHN SCOFFIN. ANGUS McCALLUM. JOHN MARWOOD. AND

ANGUS McKAY.

-AND-   PLAINTIFFS

HANNAH BELINDA MCINTYRE. ROBERT ROW. EMERSON JOHNSON

WALKER. GEORGE FRANKLIN WALKER. ALONZO WALKER. AND

FLORENCE SMITH. THE LAST THREE BEING INFANTS UNDER

THE AGE OF TWENTY ONE YEARS

DEFENDANTS

I Certify that by a vesting Order issued out of this Honorable Court

in this cause bearing date the thirtieth day of November 1887 the following

lands being composed of the East half of Lot number One in the sixth Con-

cession of the Township of North Dorchester South of the River in the

County of Middlesex and Province of Ontario and the South West quarter

of Lot "B" in the seventh Concession of South Dorchester in the County

of Elgin in the Province of Ontario were and the same are thereby vested

in John Swartout of the said Township of North Dorchester Farmer his heirs

and assigns forever for all the estate right title and interest of the

said Plaintiffs and defendants freed and discharged from all the legacies

mentioned in will of the said Johnson Walker deceased

And this Certificate is given for the purpose of registration pursuant

to the Statute in such cases made and provided

As Witness my hand and seal of office this tenth day of December one

thousand eight hundred and eighty seven.   H B Beard

Deputy Registrar at Woodstock

Document from Chancery Court records, RG 22, Series 152 (courtesy Oxford
County Registry Office)

The judicial system and its records were of course not made and arranged for ancestor-hunters. For a deeper understanding of the system and its procedures, see "Court Records As a Genealogical Resource" by Gordon Dodds, in *Readings in Ontario Genealogical Sources*.

Pioneer homestead near Renfrew, Ontario c 1913 (courtesy author)

7/ Immigration/Naturalization

1803	British Passenger Act
1828	Naturalization Registers began for non-British subjects
1865	Ships' passenger lists recorded, port of Quebec
1908	Customs and Immigration border ports of entry established
1947	Canadian Citizenship Act

A) Ships' Lists and Arrival Information

EARLY
SHIPS' LISTS

Almost everyone wants to find their emigrating family on a ship's passenger list -- tangible evidence that they did indeed endure that long and cruel voyage. It is unfortunate that most will be disappointed. Although from 1803 the British government required a ship's captain to list all passengers at his port of departure, and from 1817 his debarkation point, very few lists have been found. Those that were located appear to have been made for private purposes rather than in compliance with the 1803 Passenger Act.

SPONSORED
EMIGRATION

Some records that have turned up from the Colonial Office 1817-31 regarding subsidized emigration plans are indexed by surname at PAC. For instance there are ships' lists for some of the Peter Robinson settlers and other groups going to Lanark County.

Some of the names involved with early "mass"emigration besides **Peter Robinson** whose settlers went mainly to Lanark and Peterborough Counties are **Lord Selkirk**, whose settlement in Ontario was at Baldoon in Kent County; **Col. Thomas Talbot**, who brought emigrants to what is now Elgin County; **Timothy Rogers,** who brought Quaker settlement to York County; **Berczy's** German settlers and the **Comte de Puisaye's** French Royalists in York County; and **Joseph Brant** who led the Six Nations to the Grand River. Other major settlement undertakings included the opening of the German Company Tract in Waterloo County, the vast Canada Company territories and smaller efforts by various emigration societies that were formed in Britain and Canada to assist families to make the move. These are mentioned because in many cases historians have written articles or publications about them, and sometimes an effort has been made to compile lists of the emigrants involved. Some schemes were successful and some were not.

Some genealogical reference articles are:

- "The Irish Emigrant Settler in the Pioneer Kawarthas" by Howard Pammett in *Families*, Vol. 17, No. 4 (1978),
- "Baldoon: Success or Failure" by A.E.D. MacKenzie in *Families*, Vol. 12, No. 3 (1973),
- "Red River Colonists and Lake Erie Pioneers" by Robert A. Jones in *Canadian Genealogist*, Vol. 4, No. 2 (1982)
- "John and Catherine (Grant) Sutherland: Selkirk Settlers" by Milton Rubincam in *Canadian Genealogist*, Vol. 4, No. 4 (1982),
- "Hessian Migration to the Canada Company's Huron Tract "by Stafford Johnston in *Families*, Vol. 15, No. 4 (1976),
- "Hamilton and the Immigration Tide" by John C. Weaver in *Families*, Vol. 20, No. 4 (1981),
- "The Petworth Emigration Committee: Lord Egremont's Assisted Emigrations from Sussex to upper Canada, 1832-37" by Wendy Cameron in *Ontario History*,Vol. LXV (1973),
- "The Settlement of Manitoulin Island" by Shelley J. Pearson in *Families*, Vol. 21, No. 1 (1982).

Families, Canadian Genealogist, The Ontario Register, and *Ontario History* all contain articles too numerous to list here on the early settlement of townships and communities.

Donald Whyte's voluminous *A Dictionary of Scottish Emigrants to Canada Before Confederation* should also be consulted for information about the arrivals of over 12,000 Scots. Another book that lists hundreds of original settlers through their land grants is Coleman's *The Canada Company*. Turk's *The Quiet Adventurers* chronicles a lesser known group of Channel Islands immigrants.

Manuscript collections of the private papers of individuals involved in emigration plans can also be seen at PAC and AO. Some examples are the Selkirk Papers, Peter Robinson Papers, Berczy Papers and McNab Papers. "Land Settlement in Upper Canada, 1783-1840" by Gilbert C. Anderson in the sixteenth Department of Archives *Report* (1920) gives a very detailed history of many settlement plans.

In *Families*, Vol. 25, No. 2 (1986) there is an article called "A Selection of Lists from British military Records, Series C" by Constance E. Dods which contains extracts from that series of several 1820 lists of emigrants recorded by various emigration societies.

One well-known publication is Filby's *Passenger and Immigration Lists Index*. Originally published in three volumes, several supplements have been added. Many Canadian entries are included, but be aware that entries are only from sources that have been **published**, with the attendant possibility of transcription error. It will undoubtedly be more difficult to locate and consult the **original** source or list.

There is a group of early records on microfilm at AO under the ambiguous title "Emigrant Returns" for which the finding aid is an appendix to the Crown Lands finding aid. Surnames are listed alphabetically in the finding aid. A description of contents is found on the film itself, and consists of returns of Scottish and Irish settlers and disbanded soldiers between 1815 and 1834. The locations were the military administrations in Lanark County.

Many of the returns give property descriptions for the settler, indicating his date of arrival. For example, there is a list of ex-military settlers eligible for patents in 1822 and a list of Lanark settlers who received government "stores" or provisions for the period 1821-28.

EMIGRANT AGENTS

Emigrant Agent's Offices were created in the 1820s and 1830s along the St. Lawrence River and the Great Lakes to exercise some control over sick or indigent arrivals, and a few sources of genealogical value have survived from these "field offices". At PAC there is a card catalogue of arrivals who were provisioned by the agents in the 1840s. Almost nothing remains from the later quarantine stations in Ontario.

AO has immigration books for the port of Kingston during the 1860s.

The province of Ontario kept its own Department of Immigration for some time after Confederation, the surviving records of which are now at AO with a finding aid. For genealogical purposes, useful items might be Letterbooks 1869-1901 indexed by name, Destination Registers 1872-74, Passage Warrants 1872-88, and Applications for Refunds 1872-75 indexed by name.

LATER SHIPS' LISTS

After 1865 ships' lists are more common, at PAC on microfilm for the official ports of entry: **Quebec** from 1865 and **Halifax** from 1881. Both of these series extend on microfilm to 1919. Thousands of passengers arriving at these ports had Ontario as their final destination. The years 1865 to 1869 at Quebec are indexed by name on an old card catalogue at PAC but the catalogue is considered incomplete and inaccurate.

Otherwise, the films are arranged by port, and thereunder chronologically by year of arrival. From 1865 to 1900 there will be a list of the ships' names at the beginning of each year. For others, there are separate finding aids to consult at PAC. In Jonasson's *Canadian Genealogical Handbook* there is a conversion list for years 1865-1900 for microfilm numbers.

The actual lists vary a great deal in content, but the best will include all family members, ages, country of origin, class of travel and eventual destination. The drawback is that some individuals may have been missed in the actual count.

It must be emphasized that these lists take a long time to search, whether you do it in person at PAC or through Inter Library Loan. Obviously the search time is considerably shortened by knowing the year and month of arrival. As a research guide, PAC advises that if you are searching an eight-year period after 1900 without knowing the port of arrival it could take you well over a week to search ships arriving at the two above ports, besides arrivals at the later additional ports of Saint John, North Sydney, Vancouver and Victoria.

Ships' lists of emigrants who arrived via a non-designated official port will not be found at PAC if in fact lists were made. The only possibility is that a list might have survived at the embarkation port.

One point to remember is that depending on the time period and conditions in continental Europe, non-British emigrants very often went to a British port to transfer to a ship destined for Canada. In the earlier years few passenger ships arrived directly from continental Europe; this had changed dramatically by the end of the nineteenth century. Naturalization papers for such people may give a specific date of arrival or at least make for better guesswork (see next section of this chapter).

PAC also has copies of lists from 1906 and up until as late as 1921 in some cases for many **American** ports,only of people who declared on arrival their intention to proceed directly to Canada. Most did in fact end up in Canada, but some not for a few years following.

QUARANTINE

Contagious diseases that spread from other parts of the world to Canada via ships and their passengers made it a necessity to establish quarantine stations at ports of entry during the nineteenth century. **Grosse Ile** near Quebec City was one such location, and it has received

89

a fair amount of attention from historians. "La Grosse Ile and Its Memorials" by Thomas Dukes in *Families*, Vol. 26, No. 4 (1987) plots the various cemeteries and names on markers. See also M. O'Gallagher's *Grosse Ile Gateway to Canada 1832-1937.*

In the 1820s the Quebec *Mercury* newspaper was in the habit of publishing deaths that occurred in the Emigrants' Hospital in that city. Lists of all patients' names and their origins were printed from July 1829 to November 1830. All names were published alphabetically in the Ottawa Branch OGS *News*, Vol. 15, No. 4 (1982) and the great majority were Irish immigrants.

From 1919 records of entry are with the federal Department of Employment and Immigration, to which there are alphabetical indexes after 1920. Enquiries for access to these records should be directed to the Query Response Centre of the Department (see Appendix I).

NEWSPAPERS

Newspapers in port cities published information about ship arrivals on a regular basis. Occasionally you may see the names of passengers listed.

FINDING
AID

PAC has recently made a unified microfilm guide called *Ships' Passenger Lists and Border Entry Lists in PAC, RG 76 (Records of the Immigration Branch).* It refers to the many finding aids to all the various collections, i.e. ships lists 1865-1918 and border entry lists 1901-18. As well, PAC is producing a finding aid to ship arrivals which can be consulted by date of arrival regardless of port, by ship name, by shipowner name, and by port of departure.

BORDER
ENTRY PORTS

Up until 1908 there was what could be called "free movement" across the Canada-United States border. Between 1908 and 1918 80 border ports had been established for the inspection and recording of incoming immigrants, whether by sea or by land. The records' arrangement by ports, and the large number of ports or entry points again make searching a long task, and the researcher will likely have to start with guessing. Where the ancestor lived before and after emigration might help to determine his crossing point. The arrivals' names are arranged by month and day within each port. With the use of directories before and after the fact, you may then be able to pinpoint a more exact date. You are warned that there is as yet no nominal index to these lists, that some lists may be misfiled chronologically, or that interfiling has occurred in some port groups.

Children's names were recorded as well as adults, plus ages, nationality, occupation, mode of travel, cash on hand, former residence and intended destination. Arrivals who came by road in remote areas, and **train** arrivals will not be recorded. No passenger lists were kept for trains in Canada.

JUVENILE IMMIGRATION

Immigrant children brought to Canada in the late nineteenth and early twentieth centuries through sponsored plans have generated a separate collection at PAC, for which there is a general guide. These include groups of some familiar names like Barnardo children, Quarrier Homes children and many other like organizations.

There are three aids for searching at PAC for juvenile, or child, immigration information. A list has been made of ships that carried organized groups of children 1870-99 which provides the name of the ship and its arrival date. You must then consult the appropriate ship's passenger list or manifest, as above.

The second is a Soundex card index to children's names 1892-1932, and some of the sponsors were Barnardo, Middlemore, Macpherson, Cossar and Quarrier homes, the Salvation Army, Church of England Waifs and Strays Society, and others. Information may vary from child's name and immigration file number to name of ship he arrived on, arrival date, port, previous residence, sponsoring organization and date of inspection of his new home in Canada. The original cards were destroyed after being microfilmed.

The third is a register of "British Children Emigrated to Canada by Authority of Boards of Guardians", specifically organized by British Unions which oversaw poor-law administration under Boards of Guardians. The Canadian Immigration Branch created this nominal register which covers the time period 1878-1920. The least amount of information might only be a name and a page number that refers to a now missing register. In later years information can include the child's age, year of arrival, sponsor, name of British Union and dates of inspection in new homes. Additional remarks are entered for less than half the names regarding the child's physical condition, movements, marriage, war service and other personal notes. The original book was destroyed also, after microfilming, and apparently some damaged pages have caused loss of information on both left and right margins.

Knowing that an ancestor was sponsored by one of these groups may also lead the researcher to sources in Britain. *The Home Children* by Phyllis Harrison or Kenneth Bagnall's *The Little Immigrants* are valuable background reading. A shorter article by Bagnall, "Britain's Children Who Came to Stay" appeared in *Canadian Genealogist*, Vol. 3, No. 2 (1981). Harrison has also published lists of British addresses for specific sponsoring organizations and orphans' homes in OGS *Newsleaf*, February 1986, and in *Family Tree Magazine,* Vol. 2, No. 6 (1986). All organizations have reportedly been most helpful to genealogists.

More details on the subject of immigration can be found in the following articles: "Canadian Immigration Records of Entry in Genealogical Research" by Bennett McCardle in *OGS Seminar Annual* (1985), and in *Families*, Vol. 16, No. 4 (1977) you can read both Bryan Corbett's "Genealogical Sources in the Historical Immigration Records" and Patricia Kennedy's "Records of the Immigration Process: Pre-Confederation".

B) Naturalization and Citizenship Records

OATHS OF
ALLEGIANCE

Before 1828 an Oath of Allegiance was a requirement in the land granting process, but there was no other formal requirement of citizenship or immigration. Oaths have not necessarily been isolated as a separate collection, although the Baldwin Room of the Metropolitan Toronto Reference Library does have some. These particular ones were published by Marion Keffer in 1961 and 1963 issues of *York Pioneer*.

Since Oaths were a part of everyone's application for a Crown land grant, many are still found in documentation of Upper Canada Land Petitions (PAC and AO). Others may appear in divers places such as Township Papers or Heir and Devisee Commission Records. Names of settlers are given, as are previous residence, current residence and an identifying physical description.

NATURALIZATION
REGISTERS

Naturalization as government policy grew out of political concern about non-British immigrants and the matter of loyalty to the British crown. Sensitivity on the issue was directly influenced by the arrival of U.S.-born settlers after the War of 1812. Upper Canada naturalization registers from 1828 to 1850 are at PAC and consist of oaths or affirmations that the man had lived here for at least seven years and bore allegiance to the Crown. The law required this within seven to ten years of arrival as a means of ensuring serious intentions of residency.

These registers apply only to **non-British** subjects. If your ancestor was born in England, Scotland, Ireland or Wales he was already a natural-born British subject.

92

Donald McKenzie has prepared a nominal index to these volumes, published serially in *Families*, Vol. 18, No. 3 (1979) and Vol. 19, Nos. 1-3 (1980), with a good introduction. The index will tell you name, file year, county or district of residence and entry number. The register itself will give name, residence, occupation, signature and date.

Naturalization records made by the Department of the Secretary of State from 1854 to 1917 were destroyed, but an index at PAC remains with some genealogical information. Learning the date of naturalization can shorten the search for a ship's list. From 1867 to 1917 a new arrival had to wait three years before applying; from 1917 to 1977 he had to wait five years. After 1877 the time period again became three years.

Records made after 1915 are more detailed and give date of entry as well as occupation, residence, family members, date and place of birth. Both groups are arranged and accessed alphabetically by surname and then birthdate. At present, **only** the naturalized citizen himself has access to these records, with few exceptions. Requests for information must be submitted on a special form (from any local Citizenship Court) to the Citizenship Registration Branch in Sydney (see Appendix I).

As an oversimplification of a complex situation, Canadian citizenship became effective in 1947. **Passports** have been issued since the mid-1800s through different agencies over the years. From 1867 to 1882 and after 1909 they were a federal government jurisdiction, and some records up to 1937 are at PAC.

C) LiRaMa Collection

Although not precisely records of either entry or citizenship, this collection of Russian consular records for Canada must be mentioned. Briefly, consulates for the Russian Empire had been established in Canada just after 1900, and they continued to serve the needs of expatriates until about 1922, even after the change of government in Moscow. The consuls' surnames were Likacheff (Montreal), Ragosine (Vancouver) and Mathers (Halifax), hence the PAC's designation of the collection as LiRaMa. This should not be thought of as a purely "Russian" collection of records when you consider that immigrants from the former Tsarist Empire were also from the three Baltic states, the Ukraine, Finland, Byelorussia, Georgia, Poland, Armenia, and included groups of German Mennonites, Jews and Doukhobors.

Показаніе подъ присягой. — Sworn Affidavit.

Вопросы. / Questions.	Отвѣты. / Answers.

Російскій Гражданинъ

	Вопросы. / Questions.	Отвѣты. / Answers.
1	Имя, отчество, фамилія, званіе и вѣроисповѣданіе. First name, first name of father, name, state (peasant nobleman, commoner etc.) religion.	Victor Freiberg Otto Magistrate at Kastran
2	Губернія, уѣздъ, волость, мѣстечко, село, деревня. Province, district, county, town or village.	Kastran Village Kastran County Riga District Riga Province
3	Холостъ или женатъ, имена жены и дѣтей и мѣстожительство ихъ въ Россіи. Single or married, first name of wife & children & their full address in Russia.	married Mary Freiberg Clara Freiberg aged 5½ years wife comes from same place
4	Ближайшіе родственники и ихъ мѣстожительство въ Россіи. Name of nearest relatives and their address in Russia.	Helza Freiberg mother Kastran Riga Province
5	Отношеніе къ воинской повинности (призывной, запасной или ратникъ). Military standing (Year when has to serve for the first time, or reservist or territorial 1-st or 2-nd class).	never served in Army Left Russia when 21 years of age
6	Состоялъ ли подъ слѣдствіемъ и судомъ въ Россіи и по какому дѣлу. Whether was sentenced in Russia and for what offence.	no

Questionnaire page from LiRaMa Collection, File #6246 (courtesy National Archives of Canada)

94

How were the records generated? There are two series of files: nominal and subject. All the nominal files are indexed by surname in a PAC card catalogue. The most common reasons for an immigrant to approach the consulate were to obtain proof that he had already served in the allied Russian army -- thus avoiding being drafted into the Canadian or the Russian army during World War I -- to establish his identity for the purpose of becoming naturalized, or to obtain a passport. Occasionally some wanted help in contacting relatives in the old country or were registering in compliance with Russian civil and military regulations.

The immigrant thus produced identifying documents to the consul who kept them in a file -- birth certificates, passports, photographs and other family papers. As well, a completed questionnaire gives a more personal history of the individual with his age, exact birthplace or previous residence, religion, marital status, relatives or dependents in Russia, military service, date of departure from the Empire or arrival date in Canada, port of entry and residence after immigration. The first question asks for name of immigrant, name of his father and father's "state" which is spelled out as "peasant, nobleman, commoner, etc."!

The only drawback for most of us, having found a file, is that the questionnaire and other documents or remarks are usually in the Russian language. My grandfather's file produced a photograph, several letters in Russian, many official Russian documents, a sworn affidavit in English for purposes of naturalization, and the detailed two-page questionnaire which was answered both in Russian and in English.

The second series of subject files deals with matters like deportation and extradition, military recruitment, criminal activities, estates and inheritances, charities and family breakdowns.

The LiRaMa collection, having only surfaced in the 1980s, can now provide serendipitous family information for descendants who despaired of ever locating material behind "the Iron Curtain". However if the immigrant ancestor had no reason to see the consul, for instance if he was avoiding military registration in the Russian army, there will be no file. Further description and history of this collection was published in *Toledot: The Journal of Jewish Genealogy*, Vol. 4, No. 3 (1983) by Zachary M. Baker.

ETHNIC

PAC is the repository for the records of many Canadian "ethnic" societies and organizations. Since well before the turn of the twentieth century, Canada and Ontario became the new home for people from countries all around the world. Immigrants from **China** between 1885 and 1903 have been well documented in the Chinese Records Section, Canada Employment and Immigration Commission. Immigrants from **India, Pakistan and Sri Lanka** 1951-1965 have also been recorded in a set of registers.

Some of the records at PAC of organizations specifically related to immigration are the Canadian Baltic Immigration Aid Society, North American Baptist Immigration and Colonization Society, and British Dominions Emigration Society. Some samples of others of an ethnic nature that may or may not have been involved with immigration are as follows. Your interest along these lines would be well served by an enquiry to the Manuscript Division at PAC or an address found through the annual *Directory of Associations in Canada*.

- Czechoslovak National Association of Canada, MG 28, V 111
- Finnish Organization of Canada, MG 28, V 46
- Japanese Canadian Citizens Association, MG 28, V 7
- Maltese-Canadian Society of Toronto, MG 28, V 11
- Polish Alliance Friendly Society of Canada, MG 28, V 55
- Trans-Canada Alliance of German-Canadians, MG 28, V 4
- Ukrainian Canadian Committee, MG 28 V 9
- Zionist Organization of Canada, MG 28, V 81

8/ Municipal Records

1850	Local government became administered by towns and townships
1867	Voters' lists recorded each election year
1917	Franchise Act; Ontario women gain the right to vote
1968	Formation of regional governments

The Municipal Act of 1850 put local government in the hands of elected town or township officials. Prior to this, local judicial and municipal business was handled by District Councils 1842-49, and earlier by the District Courts of General Quarter Sessions of the Peace (see Chapter 6, Section D). At the same time in 1850 county councils "replaced" district councils although the judicial aspect was removed from their authority. Some municipal organization had existed before 1850 in the more urban centres to enable elected representatives to levy taxes for local services. The Municipal Act provided for the incorporation of these local governments.

LOCATION OF
RECORDS

The records produced by local governments and the councils were of course retained in local offices. Some years ago a concerted effort was made by AO to collect past records and most jurisdictions were co-operative in that storage space had become a problem for them. Inevitably, some early records had been destroyed or lost. In other cases the records went into private keeping or to a local repository, or were still retained at the municipal office. The end result is that AO has the most comprehensive **central** collection and continues to collect, although a local site might have what you want. The reaction of municipal staff to a visit from a genealogist may vary from congenial interest to denial of access. The latter is often caused by reluctance to hunt out old records amidst the daily business of a large corporation or ignorance of their location. If you walk into one of these offices, you cannot necessarily expect expert knowledge of their historical records or a list of their holdings. Consulting the detailed inventory at AO with its appendixes will quickly tell you what is available there for the location of your own interest.

For **addresses** of municipal offices in Ontario, see the annually published *Municipal Directory*. This includes addresses as well for local municipal agencies, school boards, health units, and others. Some of the largest municipalities or cities, such as Toronto and Ottawa, have their own **archives** dedicated to the preservation of such records, as well as ongoing records management responsibilities. See "Municipal archives and Genealogy" by Mark Walsh in *OGS Seminar Annual* (1986) and "The City of Toronto Archives" in *Families*, Vol. 17, No. 3 (1978) for discussions of these institutions.

In many counties a large **library** will have a special local history collection with possibly some original old local records; also many counties have an **archives or museum** with some original material. All these places should be considered when searching for elusive and very specific local information. Publications that contain addresses of these resource centres were mentioned at the end of the Introduction (subsection: "Researching in Resource centres").

DISTRICT COUNCIL	District council records include, as well as minutes of council meetings, correspondence and bylaws, some school papers, roads and bridges reports, poll books and land registers. These are arranged by district name.
COUNTY COUNCIL	County council records are arranged by county name and include minutes, account books, committee reports, bylaws, assessment records and possibly some militia rolls.
ASSESSMENT, COLLECTORS' ROLLS	Township and Town Council records are arranged alphabetically in the AO inventory under the appropriate county name. Included here are the usual minutes and proceedings, tax collectors' rolls, assessment rolls and poll books. Generally, few assessment and collectors' rolls have survived for the pre-1850 period, although council minutes often pre-date the Municipal Act. Sometimes an early county directory or a local history will have published an assessment roll of which the original may have disappeared.

Basically the rolls supply a landowner's name, his location and amount of tax assessed or collected in a given year. Because many have survived sequentially, they can provide a family's residence between census years. Often the age of the householder is given, this information being considered as reliable as that in a census. Town or city rolls will give a subdivision plan or street address.

Statute Labour rolls have sometimes been included with assessments. They may be some or all of the men in a community who were expected to provide roads work and maintenance. Often they consist largely of young single men who have not been assessed themselves. The rolls I have seen gave the man's name, age and residence ("at Mr. Smith's").

Page 19

Names	No. of Con	No. of Lot	Description of Lots	No. of acres cultivated	No. of acres cultivated	Horses	Oxen	Milch Cows	Young Cattle	£ s d	
Householders											
Lachlan Kennedy	10	36	ft	130	70	1	4		6	141	
James Gordon	10	37	h	80	20		2			53	
John Caulfield	9	1	ft & h	125	75	2	2	1	5	49	
Saml Ahert	9	3	ft	77	23		2	1		49	8
John Ahert	8	4	h	100				1		23	
Wm Hamilton	9	1	ft	45	35		2	2	4	62	
George H. Smith	9	3	ft	66	34	1	2	2		56	
Phillip Brimlist	9	17	ft	93	7		2	1		36	12
Wm & P. Alligan	9	16	ft & h	188	12	1	2	3	1	73	12
John McGill for Wm Alligan	9	15	ft	92	8			2		40	8
Wm McGill	9	18	h	100						20	
Patk Lynch	9	15	ft	90	10			1	1	40	
Edwd Fitzmouris	9	14	ft	90	10					42	
Henry McCaul	9	11	ft	94	6					24	16
James Smith	10	18	ft	96	3		2	1	1	41	4
Hugh Carson	9	17	h	100						20	
John Dudgeon	9	13	h	73	27	1	2	2		68	12
Lewis King	9	5	ft	52	48	2	2	3		61	8
John Isles	9	4	ft	182	18	1	2	3	5	49	8
Peter Bell	10	5	ft	81	19		2	3		52	4
Chas Willoughby	9	6	h	56	44	1	2	3	5	53	4
Kenneth McKenzie	10	17	h	95	5					24	

Sample page of 1842 Assessment for Puslinch Township, RG 21, MS 700, reel 2 (courtesy Archives of Ontario)

VOTERS'
LISTS

Voters' lists were made at the municipal level from 1867 during the years when an election was held. Information on them is scant but again they serve to locate an ancestor at a specific date and time. There is a separate finding aid at AO for voters' lists 1874-1978 with a list of the years when elections took place. It is arranged alphabetically by the name of the municipality. Municipalities often had voters' lists printed, which introduces the the chance of typographical error.

Lost in Canada? has published "Contested Elections" in Vol. 11, Nos. 3 and 4 (1985) for Halton County, Vol. 12, Nos. 1, 2 and 3 (1986) for Middlesex County, and Vol. 12, No. 4 (1986) and Vol. 13, No. 1 (1987) for Oxford County. The lists of names are petitioners opposing or endorsing an elected candidate. The petitions were originally published in *Journals of the Legislative Assembly* during the 1840s. Oddly enough, many names appear on both sides of the issue.

Some of the early appointed township positions included responsibilities for problems in local community life to do with boundary or survey disputes and agricultural livestock. They were **fence viewers, livestock valuers, pound keepers** and **path masters.** If cattle broke a fence and ran away, someone had to pen them until the owner arrived. If sheep were destroyed by wolves, they had to be evaluated for municipal reimbursement. Daily problems like this, when the municipality was involved, would be recorded in the council minutes. It is still a mark of distinction today in many rural townships to serve in these positions.

EARLY CENSUS
& OTHER LISTS

Many pre-1842 census returns are listed in the census finding aid, *Ontario Census Returns*, under a town or township name. Some are listed in the AO municipal finding aid as well. Early census and assessments for Lanark, Perth and Richmond military settlements have been published by Mildred Livingston (see Appendix II), and several OGS branches have published local lists.

Besides these, two series of district records are at AO which consist of early census returns, assessment rolls, and some combined censuses and assessments. Some local institutions may have purchased copies of them. The census returns only, not the assessments, are listed in *Ontario Census Returns* under a township name. The following are the names of the townships or municipalities and the date of the **earliest** extant list. There may be few or many additional, later, returns.

Gore District

Ancaster	1816
Beverley	1816
Big Creek Indian Lands (Grand River)	1842
Binbrook	1816
Brantford	1842
Dumfries	1818
Eramosa	1825
Erin	1824
Flamborough	1842
Galt	1850
Garafraxa	1833
Glanford	1815
Grand River Tract	1816
Guelph (town)	1829
Guelph (township)	1828
Nassagaweya	1842
Nelson	1816
Nichol	1829
Onondaga	1848
Puslinch	1833
Saltfleet	1816
Trafalgar	1816
Tuscarora	1846
Waterloo	1816
Wilmot	1831
Woolwich	1827

Niagara District

Bertie	1828
Canborough	1849
Canby's Settlement	1828
Clinton	1828
Gainsborough	1828
Grantham	1828
Grimsby	1828
Haldimand County (Grand River)	1828
Humberstone	1828
Louth	1828
Pelham	1828
Rainham	1828
Thorold	1828
Wainfleet	1828
"Unidentified"	1828

The 1828 Niagara District census, with the exception of Canborough, Canby's Settlement, Haldimand County and Rainham, has been published with a nominal index by Niagara Branch OGS.

101

9/ Education Records

1785	First school opened, at Kingston
1807	Legislation to establish a grammar school in each district
1816	Legislation for common schools
1827	King's College founded (later University of Toronto)
1847	Toronto Normal School
1849	University Act; secular University of Toronto
1850	County Boards of Education formed
1876	Royal Military College, Kingston
1960	Consolidation of rural schools

Education in Ontario has evolved into a "free" system of public schools from elementary to secondary schools, called junior high schools and high schools. A major part of any municipal budget is the portion spent for education. The earliest **grammar schools** operated on tuition fees, and thus were not accessible for the entire populace. Elementary schools were initially called **common schools**. From 1850 the administering bodies for elementary and high schools were municipally-elected local boards of education and separate (Catholic) school boards. Eventually these were consolidated into fewer separate and county boards. A few religious denominations besides Catholics operate schools by their own boards of trustees. The school year now runs from September to June although this was not always the case in early days when the agricultural season had some influence.

Papers from Boards in all parts of the province have been collected by the AO in the Ministry of Education Collection, and its finding aid is suggested as a starting place to tackle this subject. This extensive collection is divided into a **government records** section and a **private manuscripts** section. The first includes the provincial Department of Education records of meeting minutes, correspondence, bylaws, inspectors' and trustees' reports, County Board minutes, teachers' contracts and training records, some school histories and teaching experiences, and file headings for each teaching subject. Some records date from before 1840.

TEACHERS

Important here for a teacher-ancestor are the **superannuation applications** made by teachers circa 1852-1912, nominally indexed. Brant County Branch OGS has published *The First Superannuated or Worn Out Common School Teachers in Upper Canada*, extracted

Public School Teacher's Application.

INFORMATION FURNISHED BY CANDIDATES FOR CERTIFICATES.

TO THE INSPECTOR OF PUBLIC SCHOOLS,

County of *Wentworth*

Dated at *Hamilton June 2* 188 *4*

The undersigned Candidate for Examination submits the following particulars for the information of the Examiners:

1. My place of birth was *Ontario*
   (PROVINCE OR COUNTRY.)

2. My age on my last birthday was *27*

3. My Religious Persuasion is *Evangelical Association*

4. I received my training as a Teacher at *Hamilton Coll. last 2 yrs.*
   (NAME THE INSTITUTION AND THE TIME YOU ATTENDED.)

5. I hold a Certificate *First Class Grade C, non professional*
   (GIVE FULL DESCRIPTION.)

dated *1884*

granted by *Education Department*

6. My previous Certificates were *3rd Class County Board*
   (GIVE FULL DESCRIPTION.)
   2 Class Provincial, Normal School

7. My last place of teaching was *S. S. N. 2 Saugeen*

8. The number of years during which I have served as a Teacher in Ontario is *5*

elsewhere, , total *5*

9. The Testimonial (herewith submitted) of Moral Character is signed by
   Rev S. L. Umbaed

10. The Testimonials (herewith submitted) of previous successful service show that I have taught *two* years on a Third Class Certificate, *Three* years on a Second Class Certificate, and years besides.

11. I desire to compete for a *First* Class Certificate* *professional*
    (IF FOR FIRST CLASS, STATE WHAT GRADE.)

12. My optional subjects are

[Study carefully the other side and state all your Optional Subjects or Groups clearly.]

13. My Post Office Address is *Heidelberg, Waterloo Co*

Moses G. Klippel
(APPLICANT TO SIGN FULL NAME HERE.)

NOTE.—This form can be given by the Inspector to intending competitors on their application, and *must be returned to him filled up not later than the FIRST OF JUNE,* and is to be kept by the Presiding Inspector, together with the testimonials, from which, if needed, information may be given to the Department.

*A Candidate who holds an Intermediate Certificate, and now comes up for additional subjects for Class III., will produce his Intermediate Certificate and give its date and number in this application.

In the case of FIRST CLASS CANDIDATES, the Inspector will send their testimonials to the Department, with this form of application.

F. 54—5,500—19th March, 1884.

[OVER

Application for first-class teaching certificate, RG 2, Series H, Box 6 (courtesy Archives of Ontario) from annual Department of Education reports on 170 retiring teachers in 1853, 1854, 1855, 1856 and 1858.

The first training schools for teachers were called Normal Schools, and then Model Schools were opened in various counties for acquiring a different class of teaching certificate. The teacher's type of training and location of teaching experience is documented on his superannuation form. Other information given is birthplace, residence, religious affiliation, age and number of teaching years.

Just some of the other records found in this collection are Normal and Model school admission applications 1847-49 and 1869-72, third class certificates 1877-1901, examination papers 1859-79 and Toronto Normal School student registers 1847-59 and 1863-73. Some records are subject to the 100 year access restriction, depending on the current authority responsible for their original creation.

AO holds a collection of the Ontario Educational Association, 1861-1986, a professional teachers' organization, with a finding aid.

STUDENTS

Do not expect to find a lot of lists with pupils' or students' names here. There are such records as attendance rolls, reports, examinations, school registers and copybooks from about 1850 to 1910 for elementary, high and separate schools, but this is another instance where the 100 year restriction often applies. "Miscellaneous school records 1850-90" are arranged by placename location.

A second, smaller collection at AO called Education Papers has a variety of miscellaneous manuscript material on schools around the province. Each item is catalogued in the finding aid for this collection, with placenames and dates.

Little has been published, genealogically speaking, of original school records. One article that lists students is "Report of a Common School in Elizabeth(town) Township, Leeds County: 1842" in *Families*, Vol. 15, No. 3 (1976) by Lee Booth. Nipissing District Branch OGS published some students' names at schools in their area in 1906 and 1914 in *Public Relations*, August 1987, their newsletter. George W. Spragge wrote "The Cornwall Grammar School under John Strachan, 1803-1812" in *Ontario History*, Vol. 34 (1942). More information is available in the 28-volume set called *Documentary History of Education in Upper Canada* by John G.Hodgins.

Writing to a particular Board may or may not result in permission for access if the records are in AO custody; their policies also may differ on access to more current records. Certainly the Toronto Board of Education for one, will cooperate with records for nineteenth and early twentieth century student registration. Write to the Archivist, 155 College St., Toronto, Ontario M5T 1P6. **Addresses** for other Boards of Education may be found in the *Municipal Directory*.

To find something useful in the AO collection it is necessary to spend considerable time examining the finding aid and relating the locations and dates to your family. Again, if you work your way through to a local resource centre, there may or may not be some miscellaneous original school or education papers in its holdings.

Privately funded schools operate independently, and should probably be contacted in writing for information.

School examination results and awards have been printed in local newspapers since the mid-nineteenth century, usually coinciding with the end of a school term (Christmas) or year (June). In a more contemporary vein, school yearbooks are good sources for student activities, awards and a photograph and mini-commentary for the graduating classes.

COLLEGE,
UNIVERSITY

Universities and other learning institutions beyond the high school level were and are a provincial, rather than a county, concern. While in the AO collection there is a section of University of Toronto correspondence, on the whole these institutions have retained their own records. If you are searching for traces of an ancestor in this matter, your first problem may be to determine what university he attended. In the nineteenth century it is easier when you realize how few universities there were -- Queen's in Kingston; McMaster in Toronto, later Hamilton; Ottawa; Western in London; and Toronto. Most of these began as colleges and may have had earlier names. Initially the colleges were sponsored by or affiliated with organized religion. By 1964 there were fourteen universities in Ontario.

Professional faculties like medecine, divinity and law were also very few at first. Today, by comparison and as one example, there are over thirty theology and divinity schools, seminaries and bible colleges.

When you have located the right place you may find cooperation with enrollment and graduation dates, published notices or academic records. University libraries or archives are natural reference centres and tend to acquire material about or by their graduates. Their addresses are found in the *Directory of Canadian Records and Manuscript Repositories* published by the Association of Canadian Archivists. Some of the major university libraries are in Appendix I. An ancestor in a professional career might be mentioned in professional yearbooks, biographies or *Who's Who in Canada*.

College and university yearbooks are sources of biographical information about graduates, sometimes stating their future intentions. "University Yearbooks as a Source of Migration" was explored by Donald E. Read in *Families*, Vol. 24, No. 4 (1985), and to that I might add alumnae newsletters. Even the newspapers published by students, if they are held at university libraries, can be a source of extra information.

Class photograph, Grade One, St. James Public School, Thunder Bay 1946 (courtesy author)

10/ Military Records

Until the mid-nineteenth century the defense of Ontario and other Canadian provinces was provided by regular British army troops. Thus British military and government records up to this time contain much interspersed material on Canadian involvement in war and defense. To help understand and locate different types of military and defense records, you could read "An Introduction to Military Records for the Genealogist" by Jonasson in *Families*, Vol. 20, No. 4 (1981), *Searching for a Soldier in the British Army or Canadian Militia* by John H. Grenville, and "Military Sources at the Public Archives of Canada" by Carl A. Christie in *Families*, Vol. 16, No. 4 (1977). Also highly recommended is *A Military History of Canada* by Desmond Morton.

MILITIA

The local militia system existed from earliest times, but apart from participation in the War of 1812 and the Rebellion of 1837 their activity seems to have been limited to the annual muster for training. Able-bodied men between the ages of sixteen and sixty were required to serve in a militia unit, often referred to as the "sedentary" militia and usually organized on a county basis.

Muster rolls of militia units have survived for scattered counties and dates, indicating a man's name and sometimes age and home township. None of them are found in one central collection. At AO they may be catalogued under "militia" or "military" or by county holdings. At PAC, enrollment lists, muster rolls and pay lists for militia are found in various record groups according to the government or military department responsible for them at that time. Some lists and papers relating to militia have survived in private hands and will be found among private manuscript collections, such as those of a prominent man who served as a militia commander. Some lists have been published in local historical society bulletins or other local histories. Men who did not appear for the annual muster were fined, and sometimes you can see evidence on the lists that someone had bribed another man to take his place.

"The Lincoln Militia" by Albert Stray in *Canadian Genealogist*, Vol. 7, No. 4 (1985) explores what a genealogist can learn from available records. Also, J.A.C. Kennedy's "Lincoln Militia Returns 1818" in *Families*, Vol. 10, No. 2 (1971) lists names. Some other published militia returns are found in *The Ontario Register* Vol. 1, No. 3 (1968) for Hastings County, Vol. 1, No. 4 (1968) for Northumberland County, and Vol. 7, No. 1 (1983) for parts of Kent County, Vol. 3 (1970) for Thurlow in Hastings County and Rainham in Haldimand County, and Vol 2 (1969) for Prince Edward County.

OGS is preparing to publish soon Bruce Elliott's indexed compilation of all known 1828 militia lists for Upper Canada, which will be extremely useful for locating ancestors at that time.

In 1866 the active militia saw its first battle action during the Fenian raids. Later, action in the Canadian west included Ontario men when problems arose at Red river and in the Riel, or North West, Rebellion.

WAR OF 1812

Although no complete list of militia veterans is available, there is a list of 1812 war veterans who were alive in 1875 and who then applied for a government land grant. This has been reproduced by Eric Jonasson with an excellent introduction as *Canadian Veterans of the War of 1812*.

Another alternative for ancestral information is to search the Upper Canada land petitions series for a militia veteran who might have applied around 1819-20 for a land grant on the strength of his service. He would have had to supply some details of his service to be eligible. There was also a provision for these men to exchange a grant for "scrip", or money.

1837 REBELLION

British War Office records, copies of which are at PAC, include lists of some militia units 1837-50. Names of officers and men who died were printed in the 1904 *Bureau of Archives Report*. The series called **Upper Canada Sundries** at PAC and AO contain extensive references to subsequent trials of traitors, with witnesses' accounts of local meetings and skirmishes. At AO there is a separate finding aid to Rebellion of 1837 papers, including depositions and names of traitors. See "Canada's Gallant Volunteers of 1837-38: Roll Call, Winter of 1890-91" by Broughton in *Families*, Vol. 27. No. 1 (1988). There are hundreds of names of men still alive over fifty years after their service, first published in the Kingston *British Whig* in 1891.

FENIAN RAIDS

Bounty claims by veterans of this period can be found at PAC 1912-15, for those who were still living, and are indexed by surname. Information might also be sought through land petitions for militia service in the AO Crown Lands Papers, Appendix I.

RED RIVER, NORTH WEST

Pay lists for the units on duty at this time are at PAC. Claims for land grants were published in *Dominion Sessional Papers*, Vol. 5, No. 6 (1872) and Vol. 8, No. 8 (1875).

SOUTH AFRICAN WAR

Both service records for the South African War and veterans' subsequent applications for land grants are indexed at PAC under the Department of Veterans Affairs collection. These contain enlistment information such as age, physical description, occupation, name of next of kin, and address at the time of applying for land and service information. Appendix I of the Crown Lands Papers at AO can also be consulted for land petitions. In "Serving the Empire: Canadians in South Africa, 1899-1902" in *Families*, Vol. 21, No. 1 (1982), Glenn Wright describes the considerable number of records available for these men at PAC.

MEDAL REGISTERS

Medals awarded for service from the War of 1812 to the South African War are compiled on registers at PAC, with one index for the whole group.

ORIGINAL

OFFICERS' DECLARATION PAPER

oK

CANADIAN OVER-SEAS EXPEDITIONARY FORCE

QUESTIONS TO BE ANSWERED BY OFFICER

[ANSWERS]

1. (a) What is your Surname ?.. Dougall...............................

    (b) What are your Christian Names ?........................... Hector Fraser......................

2. (a) Where were you born ? (State place and country)............ Winnipeg, Manitoba................

    (b) What is your present address ?............................. 251, Bell Avenue, Winnipeg.

3.   What is the date of your birth ?............................... August 23rd., 1896.

4.   What is (a) the name of your next-of-kin ?................... Isabel Dougall

         (b) the address of your next-of-kin ?................... 251, Bell Avenue, Winnipeg.

         (c) the relationship of your next-of-kin ?........... Mother

5.   What is your profession or occupation ?......................... Clerk

6.   What is your religion ?.. Presbyterian

7.   Are you willing to be vaccinated or re-vaccinated and inoculated ?........... Yes

8.   To what Unit of the Active Militia do you belong ?......100th. Winnipeg Grenadiers.

9.   State particulars of any former Military Service............79th. Cameron Highlanders.

10.   Are you willing to serve in the

       CANADIAN OVER-SEAS EXPEDITIONARY FORCE ?........Yes

The undersigned hereby declares that the above answers made by him to the above questions are true.

_____ HDougall g _____ (Signature of Officer)

Taken on strength (place)............ Winnipeg, Man.

        (date)............ May 8th. 1916.

(Signature of Commanding Officer.)

CERTIFICATE OF MEDICAL EXAMINATION

I have examined the above-named Officer in accordance with the Regulations for Army Medical Services.

I consider him*.....Fit....................for the CANADIAN OVER-SEAS EXPEDITIONARY FORCE.

Date........May 8th............................191.6....

Place.........Winnipeg, Man.....................

*Insert here "fit" or "unfit"

                                  Capt.

                              Medical Officer.

M. F. W. 51
100m.—4-16.
H. Q. 1772. 39-917

Enlistment paper for Canadian Expeditionary Force, PAC/P-CE-706, CEF Routine Orders, World War I (courtesy National Archives of Canada)

| TWO WORLD WARS | Access to the two World War service records is now permitted through the Personnel Records Centre, Government Records Branch of PAC, to a descendant if the serviceman has been dead for twenty or more years. Proof of death must accompany any request for information **by a Canadian citizen** on the official **Access to Information Request Form**. The form is available in most Canadian post offices, libraries and government information centres, along with a guide called the *Access Register* or *Personal Information Index*. This guide should be consulted in order to state exact reference sources. |

The same Personnel Records Centre has some Imperial Gratuities files for Canadians who served with British Forces during the first World War, such as men in the RAF.

Information on Canadians who died overseas in both World Wars is available from:

Secretary-General
Canadian Agency
Commonwealth War Graves Commission
East Memorial Building
Ottawa, Ontario
K1A 0P4

Dorothy Martin has written "The Ontario Military Hospital, Orpington, England" in *Families*, Vol. 25, No. 3 (1985), with names of Canadian soldiers buried in their cemetery 1916-19.

KOREAN WAR

The Korean Veterans Association, Box 1164, Cambridge, Ontario N1R 6C9 can help with family members who died in this conflict, as they have some burial information, especially on the Commonwealth cemetery in Japan, and photographs of graves. To obtain information from them, you must know the man's name, serial number, rank, regiment and death date.

According to current government policy, military files are maintained for an indefinite period, either in a federal department or at PAC, because of their historical value. However, records of reservists,or volunteer army reserve, the modern equivalent of the old volunteer militia, are destroyed after seventy years.

NAVY

As it was for land defense in the young country, it was the Royal Navy that first supplied ships for the waterways that were so important for travel and communication. Well before the American Revolution developed, Britain had naval establishments in North America.

111

Navy Island above Niagara Falls and Detroit were two of them. Settlers were called on to serve in various capacities with the navy whenever there occurred a threat to British sovereignty. Unlike the provisions made for land grants to Loyalists who had served in militia units during the Revolution, volunteers in the provincial naval service at this time were not specifically recognized. However, there are existing petitions for land grants made by some of these men.

While PAC has copies of overseas Admiralty Office records and some collections of Royal Navy personnel records, the bulk of Royal Navy records remains at the Public Record Office in England.

Locating and searching Canadian naval records since 1910 is the same procedure as hunting army records. Informative background reading is "The Army Origin of the Royal Canadian Navy" by Lt.-Col. George Stanley in *Journal of the Society of Army Historical Research*, Vol. 32 (1954).

PROVINCIAL MARINE

The Provincial Marine grew out of the naval establishments and the provincial naval service after the American Revolution as a protective fleet on the Great Lakes and other strategic waterways. It also became the obvious mode of transportation for government and commercial supplies starting with the movement of Loyalists across the lower Great Lakes system. However, the British Admiralty took command with the Royal Navy over the Great Lakes during the War of 1812, and from then the Provincial Marine deteriorated with the growth of private shipping and navigation companies.

Records from the Provincial Marine and the Admiralty Lake Service are found at both PAC and AO in the record group of Office of the Commander of the Forces, British North America, commonly called the "C Series" and re-named the "I Series". At AO the finding aid is filed under British Military Records.

One very interesting recent development is the Descendants of the Establishments Heritage Organization, a group dedicated to research of the early naval and military establishments. Based at Box 1800, Penetanguishene, Ontario L0K 1P0, they have reconstructed the Historic Military and Naval Establishment at Penetanguishene, which flourished between 1817 and 1856, and it has become a great tourist attraction. Descendants of the men who served there, many of whom settled in Ontario, are invited to visit and to participate in the annual Descendants' Day. More than 1500 descendants have now been traced. The first two issues of *Families* in 1988 will feature articles on this subject by Gwen Patterson.

BRITISH ARMY

Because so many soldiers from the British army settled in Ontario after some service here, descendants will want to trace them through army records. British War Office records relating to Canada are at the Public Record Office in England, and PAC has microfilm copies of these. Both PAC and AO have copies of the massive military "C Series" referred to above, which has some nominal indexes. PAC also has some filmed monthly returns of officers,arranged by regiment,in their MG 13.

War Office records that give details of an individual's military service are more numerous for officers than for enlisted men. It is essential that you know the name of your ancestor's regiment to begin any research. Military and regimental histories will be useful for learning the postings in Ontario of various regiments and battalions. Arthur White's *A Bibliography of Regimental Histories of the British Army* can help with book titles. Both the Royal Canadian Military Institute and the Metropolitan Toronto Central Reference Library have extensive collections on military subjects.

When a regiment has been determined, some War Office records can be ordered on microfilm through an LDS Library. Soldiers' documents can include enlistment information with a physical description and that all-important parish of birth.

From the days after the American Revolution, discharged British soldiers who wished to remain or return and settle here were allowed a land grant for their service, as mentioned in Section A, Chapter 5. Since they had to supply some proof of service for this privilege, Upper Canada Land Petitions may be one search that will determine the name of a man's regiment.

"The Forgotten Veterans of 1812" by Albert M. Fortier, Jr. in *Canadian Genealogist*, Vol. 5, No. 2 (1983) refers specifically to discharged soldiers of the Tenth Royal Veterans Battalion who chose to settle in Canada after that war, and lists 200 men.

GERMAN MERCENARIES

Hired soldiers of Germanic background formed part of the King's regular army forces during the Revolution. Hundreds of them became military claimants for land grants when the war ended.

Besides tracing them through land petitions, a descendant researching a Germanic name would do well to consult DeMarce's *German Military Settlers in Canada, After the American Revolution.* Extensive research in Canadian, German and British archives has produced a treasury of information on the alphabetically-arranged names.

CHELSEA
PENSIONERS

Some wounded soldiers who were pensioned out of the army after spending time in Chelsea Hospital, London, eventually came to Ontario over several years starting about 1830 through a government plan. They exchanged or commuted their pensions for a grant of money or land. Many did not adapt to a farming life on their land and returned to Britain. Those who stayed can be sought again through Upper Canada Land Petitions. Previous information about them can be searched in **Chelsea Hospital's Regimental Registers of Pensioners** through the LDS Library, or through regular War office records, all arranged by regiment. See the excellent article "Searching Chelsea Pensioners in Upper Canada and Great Britain" by Barbara B. Aitken in *Families*, Vol. 23, Nos. 3 and 4 (1984) which lists sources for research and names of 654 pensioners who were alive in 1839.

LOSSES
CLAIMS

Claims for losses during war activities deserve a brief mention although they are not actual military records. After the American Revolution a British Claims Commission received applications from Loyalists for compensation of losses suffered during that period. This will be discussed in Chapter 11 on Loyalist sources.

During the War of 1812 and the Rebellion of 1837 some civilians had property destroyed by invading forces, or had goods seized by the defenders to supply the fighting troops. At PAC you can find claims for losses for both these events. For the War of 1812 there is a nominal index on microfilm; Rebellion losses are not indexed. AO has a copy of the War of 1812 losses claims 1813-48. Some claims may also be found there in manuscript material catalogued under county names, e.g. Hastings (County) Rebellion Claims 1837-45.

See "The War of 1812 Losses Claims, A Note on Sources for Genealogical Research" by Larry L. Kulisek in OGS *Seminar Annual* (1986). *Lost in Canada?* has published a series of "Rebellion Losses" covering many districts of the province in Vol. 9, Nos. 2, 3 and 4 (1983) and Vol. 10, Nos. 1-4 (1984).

11/ Loyalist Sources

REFERENCE
DATES

1783	Treaty of Separation
1783-84	Major influx of Loyalists to Canada
1789	Lord Dorchester's Resolution accompanied by the UE mark of honour note
1796	Governor Simcoe required Loyalists to register
1799	Executive Council UE List began
1896	Formation of the United Empire Loyalists' Association

Loyalist records as such are not a separate group of documents. Evidence of Loyalist ancestry is found in the usual documentation processes for any ancestor, such as land records, church records or military papers. The term "Loyalist" is used here as the popular expression of the designation **UE**. It refers to the person entitled by government recognition to the use of the initials UE (Unity of Empire) because of his adherence to the Crown during the American Revolution and subsequent removal to Canada.

To this day there is some disagreement among scholars as to the definition of "adhered to the Unity of Empire" and therefore the qualifications of Loyalists. A Loyalist has been interpreted as a person who resided in the American Colonies prior to the war with Britain, who joined the British forces ("the Royal Standard") in some capacity before 1783, and who experienced some loss of property, goods or life. Widows or children of men who died in the British cause, before or after coming to Ontario, often received land grants that recognized the men as Loyalists. It seems that the Loyalists themselves rarely practiced the use of "UE" after their names, although such was used by the government on land petitions.

LOYALIST
LISTS

There is no definitive, accurate list of Loyalists. Those who came to this newly-created province were initially given free land grants commensurate with their military rank and the number of dependants. As the District Land Boards issued certificates for land, they began to realize the need to keep track of Loyalist claimants. From 1796 the Executive Council kept a list as an attempted registry of Loyalists, based on the district rolls. Another list was created by the Crown Lands Department from many other sources. The eventual results were the **Executive Council UE List** and the **Crown Lands or "Old" UE List,** both of which had been changed well into the nineteenth century.

115

Many settlers arriving later than the end of the war in 1783 were claiming UE benefits. Some of these were called **Late Loyalists** who arrived after the first proclaimed limit of arrival of 1789; **Treasury Loyalists** who had spent time as pensioned refugees in England after the Revolution; and **Associated Loyalists** who had served with a military unit not attached to a regular army regiment. Intended to be excluded from the lists were Quakers who could not conscientiously bear arms, military claimants who were regular army soldiers, and children of Loyalists who received grants in their own names.

In 1798 another stipulation was added to the free land privilege, that grants would only be extended to those resident in Upper Canada before 1798. Thus we find two major lists which do not coincide because of the constant applications for free land, interpretation of qualifications, and periodic additions and removals from the lists.The **Crown Lands Old UE List** contains some 6,000 names, about half of them non-qualified claimants. Nevertheless this is still a source for many early settlers. The **Executive Council UE List** is considered the more accurate source with less than 3,500 names, although it is not complete.

Both lists are accessible at PAC and AO.Generation Press intends to publish the Executive Council UE List with a lengthy introduction and explanation by Elizabeth Hancocks, C.G. and former Dominion Genealogist for the United Empire Loyalist Association. The list shows the man's name and district of settlement.

MILITARY
LISTS

Muster rolls of the Loyalist Corps (the term "corps" is similar to the army "regiment") were taken at different times from their formation until disbandment after the Treaty of Separation. The Corps were formed from volunteer colonial residents as support troops for the British army. For our purposes those who settled in Ontario were disbanded around the Montreal and Niagara areas.

Some of these original lists are found within the Haldimand Papers at PAC or among the military "C Series" at PAC and AO. E. Keith Fitzgerald has prepared lists of over 2,000 Loyalist family names from several sources in the Haldimand Papers in *Loyalist Lists,* published by OGS.

Rolls of the Provincial (Loyalist) Corps, Canadian Command, American Revolutionary Period by Mary B. Fryer and Lt.-Col. William A. Smy is a consolidation of many lists. The authors have chosen lists of the major corps at the most complete size of each, which range from 1781 to 1784. Not all corps are shown in this book, and information varies on each man from nothing other than name, to birthplace (N.B. meaning North Britain), age, length of service and his height. If previous residence in the colonies is not given, you can get closer to the truth about your man with some research on where his corps was raised. It could happen that your ancestor is not on the particular list you see. If you think or know he participated, you may have to search out lists made at a different time. Highly recommended is Fryer's companion volume *King's Men, the Soldier Founders of Ontario* and the detailed sources in its footnotes. Elinor K. Senior wrote "Loyalist Regiments After the American Revolution" in *Canadian Genealogist*, Vol. 2, No. 1 (1981) with accompanying maps showing "refugee paths" and settlement areas of Loyalist Corps.

Corps names in connection with an ancestor that will alert you to possible Ontario Loyalist ancestry follow. These are corps that were associated only with the **Canadian or Northern Command:**

Provincial Corps of the British Army in 1783

Royal Highland Emigrants
King's Royal Regiment of New York
Butler's Rangers
Loyal Rangers
King's Rangers

Older Units Amalgamated into the Loyal Rangers

King's Loyal Americans
Queen's Loyal Rangers
Loyal Volunteers
McAlpin's

Unincorporated or Associated Units

Joseph Brant's Volunteers
Loyal Foresters
Detroit Volunteers
Claus' Rangers
Major Van Alstyne's
Captain Grass'

Besides the above, and some localized militia service, there were volunteers who served the British cause in the Secret Service, the Provincial Marine and the Indian Department.

A very important publication must be mentioned here although it is a secondary source. William D. Reid's *The Loyalists in Ontario, The Sons and Daughters of the American Loyalists of Upper Canada* is a compendium of Loyalist families based on the Orders-in-Council (OC) issued to children of UEs. An index to all stray names was added to the 1973 re-publication. The OC sources unquestionably provide the names of fathers who were considered Loyalists. The book's drawbacks lie in that the re-structured families do not necessarily include all children because some did not apply for land grants, some Loyalists will not appear at all, and some names or generations have been confused within or between families. The book can nonetheless be used as a valuable guide to primary sources.

PETITIONS

Petitions from Loyalists seeking their free land grants are found among Upper Canada Land Petitions (see Section B, Chapter 5). However, many were too busy with re-settling to petition for a patent in exchange for their original certificates from the Land Boards, or to petition as required to have their names placed on the UE list, and many died without having done either.

By far the majority of Loyalist land petitions are for their children (SUE and DUE grants). From 1787 each son and daughter of a Loyalist was entitled to a free 200 acre land grant on reaching the age of majority, which can be a helpful clue to their ages at the date of the petition. Daughters often applied soon after marriage. Whereas the UE himself would give some evidence in his petition for his claim, such as which corps he had served with, a son or daughter was required to identify the father by name with some witnesses' affidavits to support the relationship and his or her identity.

The most important point to look for on a petition is whether the petition was approved or "recommended". Some were not approved for lack of evidence from a Loyalist about his military service; some were denied because the man had arrived here after the original deadline of 1789. Some children's petitions were not recommended because the father's name was not found on the UE list. On the outside of each petition the government made several notes regarding their investigation of the claim. As these Loyalist grants were made without fees it was another reason for the government to eliminate unqualified people and keep their revenue for office fees, which all other applicants for free land had to pay.

It is the outside of the petition which tells whether the petitioner was successful. The term "recommended" is

118

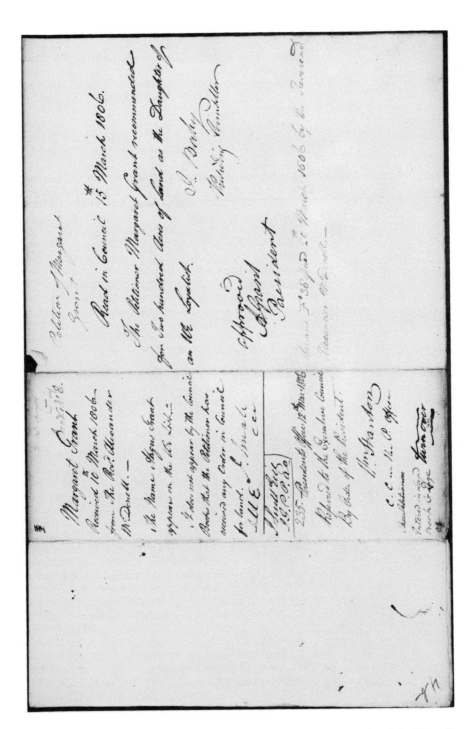

The back of a UE petition 1806, Upper Canada Land Petitions, RG 1, L3, G Bundle 8/4 (courtesy Archives of Ontario)

nearly always used to designate Loyalist recognition, and the UE initials will identify a Loyalist. Too many people have ignored the **outcome** of the petition and assumed Loyalist connections without complete research.

Having said that and making it sound a straightforward matter, there are cases where people persisted in petitioning after having been denied Loyalist status or land grants. The complexities and motives of government regulations and qualifications which changed over the years are not fully understood. The best advice when encountering a petition that was not recommended is to search the Upper Canada Land Petitions index for all occurrences of the surname, e.g. your ancestor may have made more than one petition and they may have been indexed by different spellings. Ultimately one petition may have been successful. If a son or daughter was turned down, search for petitions from other siblings to get a fuller picture.

An example of the confusion that can arise during Loyalist research is that of two children of a sergeant "with Burgoyne's" who petitioned for free land grants. The father had died in a battle in New York, and his widow fled to Canada with the two children. In 1789 the son applied for a 400-acre land grant as the son of "a noncommissioned officer in His Majesty's service". No response to this request was found with the microfilmed papers. In 1791 the son applied for an additional grant, saying that he had previously received 200 acres. His motive could have been that a sergeant may have expected a larger grant than a private, or that the widow as well as the son was entitled to a 200-acre grant each, although he does not specify. This second petition was rejected, but no reason was stated. In 1797 the son tried again, adding that neither his father nor his mother had ever applied for a land grant. This third petition was recommended with the father designated as UE. In 1800 the sergeant's daughter petitioned for her 200-acre grant as the daughter of a Loyalist and the request was denied because her father was "not on the UE List"! Perversely, an accompanying affidavit from a local Justice of the Peace said that she had previously received a 100 acre grant on the strength of her father's death in British service. Although this previous petition is missing, it must have designated the father as UE. Her intention may have been to increase the size of her grant from 100 acres to the usual 200. She did not apparently petition again.

REFUGEE
LISTS

Before the Revolution ended some refugees and families of Loyalist fighting men had arrived on the

Canadian side of the Niagara River to await the outcome. Others had trekked to Machiche on the St. Lawrence River near Sorel, or across the river from Detroit, or to Carleton Island, all areas of the British military establishment.

Some available lists from this period for provisioning and caring for the refugees have been published in Fitzgerald's *Loyalist Lists* and his article "Loyalist Stragglers in Montreal, September-October, 1784" in *Families*, Vol. 24, No. 1 (1985). Some others are "Loyalist Victualing Lists of the Niagara Area, 1786" by Robert Halfyard in *Families*, Vol. 24, Nos. 2 and 4 (1985), also published separately by the Niagara Branch OGS, and George Neville's "Returns of the Asylum at (Fort) William Henry for Loyalist Invalids" in *Families*, Vol. 16, No. 3 (1977).

CLAIMS FOR LOSSES

Loyalist Claims for Losses, perhaps the only "real" records created for this group, were heard by a British government Commission which convened at various cities in Canada and in London, England. The records groups **Audit Office 12 and 13** (PAC and AO) include evidence submitted for compensation of land and goods which the claimant owned before the Revolution. A researcher can find details of an individual's residence and possessions in the American colonies, length of residence there, perhaps birthplace if overseas, occupation, number of dependants, when he joined the Royal Standard and residence at the date of the claim. Supporting statements came from previous neighbours and character witnesses. Some claims include names of relatives and relationships. American documents of confiscation of property and forfeiture of estates can be found among Audit Office 13.

Once again, not all Loyalists made application to the Commission, for various reasons, mostly a matter of distance or expenditure. Some applied through an agent such as **John Porteous** or **Alexander Ellice** (their manuscript papers at PAC). Also not everyone who applied for compensation was deemed a Loyalist, so acceptance of a claim is needed as primary evidence of Loyalist ancestry. Acceptance or rejection of a claim is not always evident in the Audit Office papers and other sources such as land petitions must be searched. Further evidence may be found in American State records of confiscations, forfeitures and prisoners' lists. One useful publication is Maryly Penrose's *Mohawk Valley in the Revolution: Committee of Safety Papers and Genealogical Compendium*.

A List of Joseph _____ Lands, Goods and Chattels

	£		
_____ of Land 90 acres cleared	760		
_____	170		
1 Barn	60		
3 Horses	27		
1 Colt 2 years old	6		
2 Colts 1 year old	10		
1 Yoke of Oxen	20		
4 Cows & Calves	27	0	
2 two year old Steers	10		
3 year old	7	10	
2 three year old Heifers	10		
23 Sheep	10	0	
15 Store Hogs	17	16	
9 Iron ___ to a Harrow	2	5	
3 Axes	1	4	
3 Hoes	"	13	
1 Draft Chain and Hammer	1	4	
1 Pair of Coopers adze	"	6	
1 Hand Saw		10	
1 Pr of Plough Irons and Plough	2		
1 Scythe and Tackling	"	16	
2 Bells Rings	"	4	
1 Cleer and Pen 1 Grindstone 1 Yoke & Irons 1 Ox Hd 2	12	
1 Pr Snow Shoes 1 Saddle 2 Bridles & a Pan and Hid 4	6	

Carried over

A formal list of claims, Audit Office 12, Vol. 33, MS 708, reel 10 (courtesy Archives of Ontario)

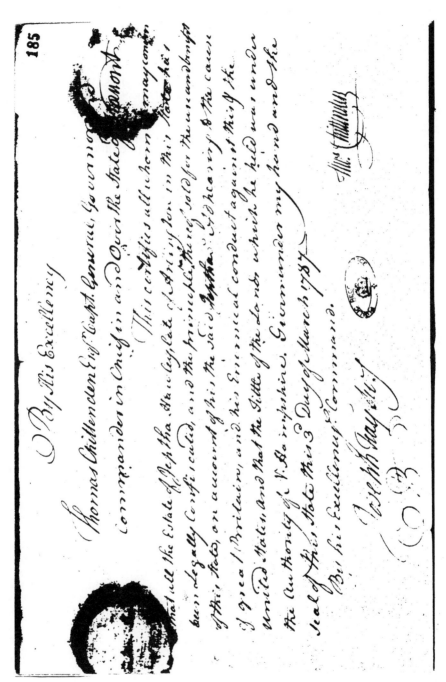

Confiscation document 1787, Audit Office 13, Bundle 13, MS 708, reel 49 (courtesy Archives of Ontario)

There are at least four publications of Claims but none is comprehensive: Antliff's *Loyalist Settlements, 1783-1789, New Evidence of Canadian Loyalist Claims* (Audit Office 12); the *Bureau of Archives Report, 1904* (Audit Office 12); Coldham's *American Loyalist Claims, Vol. 1* (Audit Office 13); and Egerton's *The Royal Commission of the Losses and Services of American Loyalists, 1783-1785*. The Antliff volume was published by AO through the Ontario Ministry of Citizenship and Culture (now Culture and Communications), and is available alone (with a surname index to the new material as well as to the *Bureau of Archives Report, 1904*) or as one of three inter-related parts of an Ontario bicentennial memorial publication. The other two parts are a microfiche reproduction of the *Bureau of Archives Report, 1904* and a portfolio of settlement location maps, samples of land granting documents and contemporary sketches.

Other sources for information on Loyalist ancestors are those previously discussed in Chapter 5 on land records, especially Heir and Devisee Commission records. Any records group of data sources for early settlers will also apply to Loyalists.

Two of the best guides to consult on the subject are Elizabeth Hancocks' "Resources for Loyalist Research" in *OGS Seminar Annual* (1984) and Patricia Kennedy's *How to Trace Your Loyalist Ancestors* published by Ottawa Branch OGS. Audrey and Robert Kirk's presentation "Approaches to U.E. Loyalist Research" in *Readings in Ontario Genealogical Sources* gives more background on UE history and sources. Norman Crowder relates the steps he followed in tracing his own ancestry in "More About the Loyalists in Ontario" in *Families*, Vol. 23, No. 3 (1984). References to further literature on Loyalists can be found in Appendix II. *OGS Seminar Annual* (1984) dealt heavily with many aspects of Loyalist sources and life.

INDIAN
LOYALISTS

Special mention can be made of reference to Indian participation as Loyalists which has not received widespread attention. "The Indian Loyalists: Their Place in Canadian History" by Helen C. Robinson appears in *OGS Seminar Annual* (1984) and "The Loyalists and the Six Nations Indians in the Niagara Peninsula" by Wilbur H. Siebert is in *Proceedings and Transactions of the Royal Society of Canada*, Vol. 9 (1916).

Both Fryer in *King's Men* and Allen in *Loyalist Literature* devote some space to Indian Loyalists. Robert S. Allen's *The British Indian Department and the Fron-*

tier in North America, 1755-1830 includes an annotated list of Indian leaders. Penrose's *Indian Affairs Papers, American Revolution* contains almost 400 pages of information.

An even less-treated subject is **French-Canadian Loyalists**, addressed by John P. DuLong in "French-Canadian and Acadian Loyalists" in *OGS Seminar Annual* (1986).

UEL
ASSOCIATION

The United Empire Loyalist Association of Canada is firstly a lineage society of UE descendants who must prove their pedigrees in order to be called UE today, and a prime requirement is allegiance to the Crown which in effect means that American citizens are not eligible. Secondly it includes affiliate membership for a proven descendant who cannot swear allegiance to the Crown, and thirdly, associate membership for anyone who is interested in history or research of Loyalists and the aims of the Association. Several local branches hold regular meetings in different Ontario cities, and have published family histories or genealogies of Loyalists in their regions.

Applications with pedigrees are processed by a local and by the Dominion genealogist. Relationships from one generation to another must be documented by standard genealogical methods, and proofs of a Loyalist ancestor must come from as many primary sources as possible, as described in this chapter.

The Toronto Branch of the Association published, as their bicentennial project in 1984, *Loyalist Lineages of Canada 1783-1983* which contains all the proven pedigrees received by the Association from 1970 to 1982. If you can prove connection to one of these lines by studying the book or contacting the Association it means that proof of the Loyalist ancestor is already on file and that part of your research has been done.

The bicentennial of the province and of the Loyalists in 1984 produced increased activity in primary research sources and a wide range of publications on Loyalists. The UEL Association publishes *The Loyalist Gazette* and a detailed index 1963-83 is now available from its Victoria Branch. Genealogical queries during these years are also part of the index. The *Gazette* was preceded by *Annual Transactions of the UEL Association of Canada* which began publishing in 1897.

An ongoing research project at PAC is called "The King's Names", sponsored by the Sir Guy Carleton Branch of the UEL Association. This project entails the indexing of all names in British Headquarters Papers (previously called the Carleton Papers) 1775-83 that include petitions to the Commander, much correspondence, reports, and lists of evacuation, assistance and pensions of refugees. Enquiries can be directed to John E. Ruch, Chairman of the Project Committee, 71 Somerset St. W., #1805, Ottawa, Ontario K2P 2G2.

Forfeiture document 1793, Audit Office 13, Bundle 13, MS 708, reel 49 (courtesy Archives of Ontario.

12/ Additional Records and Sources

This chapter became a catch-all for some records and sources that do not fit into the so-called basic record groups, or that are uncommonly used or accessible. Perhaps appealing to or useful to a small percentage of genealogists, they may be considered as intermediate or advanced research sources. Some are also very recent sources and because of their"modern" nature may not be easily accessible. There is no particular order to their placement in this chapter.

BUSINESS RECORDS

At AO in the *Preliminary Inventory of the Provincial Secretary* is some description of their holdings regarding charters and letters patent to business firms in the province. **Partnership records** are among this group and they exist from differing dates for many areas up to modern times. They can tell when a partnership was formed, when and if it dissolved and who the principals were, with addresses. They are more accessible for York County and Toronto than for other areas.

"Tracing a Family Business History" by David Bellhouse appeared in *OGS Seminar Annual* (1984) advising on universally applicable techniques. Of course **business directories** are a prime target in the search. One of the earliest for total provincial coverage is Wilson's reproduction of *Directory of the Province of Ontario, 1857.* However, it does not include every single business and professional person at that time.

Dun and Bradstreet Reference Books from 1864-1978 are in a collection at AO. They contain credit ratings and other information on commercial, business, and manufacturing companies throughout Canada, as well as banks and trust companies.

Guide to Archives in the Toronto Area and *Directory of Canadian Records and Manuscript Repositories* both list some banks and life insurance companies that have archives: **Bank of Nova Scotia, Toronto-Dominion Bank, Crown Life Insurance** and **London Life Insurance**. Their business records have limited genealogical application depending on accessibility to employment or personnel files. Appointments to see their material must be made in advance. For the possibility of obtaining information from life insurance application forms, you would have to contact directly the appropriate company and ask about their policy in this regard.

NO 7084— C.P.
ENT'D & REG'D
19TH APR. 1912—
—AT10-28 A.M.

DY. REG'R.

PROVINCE OF ONTARIO.) WE, HARRY LEVINTER, NATHAN WALL AND HARRY HERMAN,—OF THE
COUNTY OF YORK.   ) FIRM CARRYING ON BUSINESS AS GENERAL MERCHANTS AND PROPRIET—
ORS OF A SMALL— WARE STORE AT NUMBER 306 AND 308 QUEEN STREET, WEST TORONTO, UNDER
THE NAME FIRM AND STYLE OF THE "WESTERN FAIR," DO HEREBY CERTIFY1 THAT THE SAID
PARTNERSHIP WAS ON THE 13TH DAY OF APRIL 1912 DISSOLVED. WITNESSOUR HANDS AT TORONTO
THIS 13TH DAY OF APRIL A.D. 1912—

WITNESS.—
* ABRAHAM COHEN.

* NATHAN WALL.
* HARRY LEVINTER.
* HARRY HARMAN.

——————————————————————————

SCHEDULE.—

NO 7085— C.P.
ENT'D & REG'D
20TH APR. 1912—
—AT 11-30 A.M.

DY. REG'R.

DOMINION OF CANADA;—) THE UNDERSIGNED CECIL HORATIO GOOLD, ARTHUR BROOKS, THOMAS
TO WIT.   ) MCGREGOR SIBBALD, OF THE CITY OF TORONTO IN THE COUNTY OF YORK;
AND PROVINCE OF ONTARIO. HEREBY CERTIFY THAT WE HAVE CARRIED ON AND INTEND TO CARRY
ON TRADE ANDBUSINESS AS DEALERS IN CORKS, AND BOTTLERS SUPPLIES ETC. AT THE CITY OF
TORONTO INTHE COUNTY OF YORK AND PROVINCE OF ONTARIO IN PARTNERSHIP WITH EACH OTHER UNDER
THE FIRM OF ONTARIO CORK COMPANY, AND THAT THE SAID PARTNERSHIP HATH SUBSISTED SINCE THE
FIRST (1ST) DAY OF JANUARY A.D.1912— AND THAT THE SAID CECIL HORATIO GOOLD, ARTHUR
BROOKS, THOMAS MCGREGOR SIBBALD, ARE AND HAVE BEEN SINCE THE SAID DAY THE ONLY MEMBERS OF
THE SAID PARTNERSHIP. WITNESSOUR HANDS AT THE CITY OF TORONTO INTHE SAID COUNTY OF YORK;
THIS 20TH DAY OF APRIL A.D. 1912—

WITNESS.—
* ALBERT A BROOKS.

* ARTHUR BROOKS.
* CECIL HORATIO GOOLD.
* THOMAS MCGREGOR SIBBALD.

Entry from York County Partnership Record Book, Companies Division, RG 55,
MS 605 reel 37 (courtesy Archives of Ontario)

Information on past employees of **Bell Canada** whose telephone network covers Ontario may be obtained from Historical Service, Bell Canada, Room 820, 1050 Beaver Hall Hill, Montreal, Quebec H2Z 1S4. Similarly **Eaton's of Canada**, the nation's largest retail employer, maintains an archives at Yorkdale Shopping Centre, 3401 Dufferin St., Toronto, Ontario M6A 2T9. **Steel Company of Canada (Stelco),** another large employer, has an archives in Hamilton with minutes, correspondence, annual reports and the like.

The **Maclean-Hunter** collection at AO (1887-1977) consists of correspondence, minutes, reports, etc. of that publishing conglomerate, with a separate finding aid. The **Lambton Loan and Investment Company Papers** at AO (1835-1977) provide some information on borrowers and repayments, but most ledgers such as those for mortgages are restricted.

"Business, Corporate, University and Municipal Archives: Summary of Panel Presentation" appeared in *Readings in Ontario Genealogical Sources.*

OCCUPATIONS

Some pay lists for what have become national **railway companies** are held at PAC in the Federal Archives Division. Service as a **federal government employee**, in the **Royal Canadian Mounted Police (RCMP),** air and nautical **pilots,** and **merchant seamen** created records of which many are also now at this division of PAC. Access to them is governed by the most current legislation on privacy and access to information. Researchers are urged to consult a copy of the *Access Register* to personal information banks at a local federal government office, a post office or library. This will be the most up-to-date listing of accessible federal information banks and includes the appropriate form for requesting information.

Information on **merchant seamen** and their ships can be found in *History of the Great Lakes* and in the quarterly *Inland Seas*, published by the Great Lakes Historical Society. *Canadian Coastal and Inland Steam Vessels, 1809-1930* by John M. Mills lists names of ships but not their captains and crew.

Other **police** records include those of the Ontario Provincial Police, which was organized in 1909 and from which the records date. Some constables had been appointed even earlier in 1877 and 1884 for peace keeping on a province-wide basis. There is a range of 25 to 50 years' restriction on the records in AO custody: force members 1917-21, applications 1909-25, awards 1946-76 and investigation files. The most genealogically informative would be Series E of the finding aid -- personnel and training, and criminal investigation records and reports.

Ancestors in professions like **law**, the **ministry**, **medicine** and **engineering** may be sought in several ways. University records, yearbooks and alumnae news letters are one source (see Chapter 9). The *Dictionary of Canadian Biography* is a massive scholarly effort to document the lives of prominent and not-so-prominent citizens from the beginning of the province. Each volume encompasses ten years or more with entries by the person's year of death. Most professions also have yearbooks devoted to biographical information. Some records from now defunct legal firms in Ontario have been deposited with AO.

Surveyors left diaries and field notebooks of their often lonely journeys through the wilderness. They can occasionally be very informative for someone seeking a pioneer ancestor who was ahead of officially recognized township settlement. Some surveyors would note names of men they were able to hire locally as axemen, labourers and cooks. At AO these early records are found within the Crown Lands finding aid. Additional information may be available from the General Manager, Surveying Services, Room 3446, Whitney Block, Queen's Park, Toronto, Ontario M7A 1W3.

"Canadian Post Office Records for the Genealogist" by Donald E. Read in *Families*, Vol. 25, No. 3 (1986) is a helpful article for information on a **postmaster** ancestor. Local directories nearly always list postmasters, **municipally elected and government employees, judicial functionaries,** and **officials or trustees of local organizations.**

A series at PAC accessible by a name card index in the reference room is called the "Old S Series" and relates to applications for a variety of licences, commissions, pardons, appointments and bailiff records in the Canadas. Once a relevant card is found, however, it may be very difficult to locate the original source due to outmoded methods of indexing and cataloguing. Help is available in a guide to the series.

VOYAGEURS,
FUR TRADERS

Voyageurs or **fur traders** quite often pre-dated the official settlement of this province, with their main centres or route posts at Montreal, Detroit and Michilimackinac. Most early men in this business were French Canadians or Scots. Searching for records of genealogical information in this period before churches and civil administration were established can be a

130

lengthy and frustrating job. Some understanding of the water routes they used and the early British forts or outposts is essential to tracking where and when a man might have left records and a family. See "Early Traders and Trade Routes in Ontario and the West" by E.A. Cruikshank in *Transactions of the Canadian Institute* (1891-2).

Under the military administration of these places it is possible that chaplains were present to perform baptisms, marriages and burials, of civilians as well as soldiers, and such records would no doubt be filed with the commanding officer and later to his superiors in England. Some records from the fur trading era like those of the North West Company or the American Fur Company, and papers of individuals like Simon Fraser are held at PAC but they are not large collections.

In *OGS Seminar Annual* (1986) James L. Hansen wrote "Tracing the Voyageurs" which applies specifically to French Canadian Catholic ancestry. Descendants of voyageurs in Ontario can be found in pockets along the Great Lakes shores. Hilde Beaty's very interesting article "Louis and Toussaint Charbonneau" in *Families*, Vol 26, No. 1 (1987) illustrates how some of these men travelled all over the continent, and how records were found in Detroit. Detroit was part of British territory for so long that other useful publications are Donna Valley Stuart's *Michigan Censuses 1710-1830, Under the French, British, and Americans* and the Detroit Society for Genealogical Research's *The Genealogy of the French Families of the Detroit River Region 1701-1936*. Fur Trade Papers c1812-1885 at AO include some private and some company papers.

HUDSON'S BAY COMPANY

This fur trading company was involved with North American exploration and trade from 1670. Accessions in the Hudson's Bay Company (HBC) archives in Winnipeg now include 300 years' worth of records. Considerable activity has taken place in the last few years,and continues, to preserve, catalogue and microfilm.

Some of the employees or "servants" served in the province of Ontario through their Northern and Southern Departments, and numerous records can be consulted that tell name of employee, age, occupation, wages and location of HBC employment. In an appendix to her presentations on the HBC in *OGS Seminar Annual* (1983) Judith Beattie lists nineteen HBC posts in Ontario with the types and dates of records available for them. One of her articles, "The Hudson's Bay Company - A Presence in Northern Ontario", uses ten men as examples of what the records will reveal. Another reference article is "The Hudson's Bay Company Archives"by Mark Walsh in *Families*, Vol. 26, No. 1 (1987). Surviving stones from "Two James Bay Cemeteries" were reproduced by John A. English in *Families*, Vol. 23, No. 1 (1984).

A great deal of the HBC collection is available from their archives through Interlibrary Loan on microfilm. The archives' address is in Appendix I.

PRISON
RECORDS

Some records are available at both AO and PAC. At AO in the *Preliminary Inventory of the Ministry of Correctional Services* are found jail files for inmates 1939-57, probation and parole files, adult and juvenile case files, and records for industrial schools, jails, detention centres and industrial farms. At this time there is a standard 30-year restriction on personal information, and a few records are closed altogether.

By 1850 there were at least eight jails in the province. A few noteworthy milestones were the opening of Kingston Penitentiary in 1835, the Ontario Reformatory for Boys at Penetanguishene in 1859, and in 1880 the Andrew Mercer Reformatory for Females.

Records from Kingston Penitentiary 1835-1938 are now at PAC with microfilm copies at Queen's University and the Correctional Service Canada Penal Museum, both in Kingston. Personal information about inmates from the prison registers includes labour, discipline,medical treatment, classification, escapes and releases. "Return of Convicts at the Penitentiary 1st October 1847" was featured in *Lost in Canada?*, Vol. 13, Nos. 3 and 4 (1987) as extracted from a *Journal of the Legislative Assembly* of 1848. Besides names, information is often given on age,height, physical description, where sentenced and type of crime, length of term or date of release, and his convict number. The first part lists well over 400 names of incoming and discharged prisoners; the second consists of a slightly lesser number of convicts who were still serving sentences in 1847. For reference, see also *Pioneer Crimes and Punishments in Toronto and the Home District* by James E. Jones.

Another collection is the Industrial Schools Association of Toronto 1884-1938 at AO. The schools were originally established to rehabilitate unruly, wandering or beggar children.

HOSPITALS

The AO has custody of hospital records and registers for about a half dozen general hospitals throughout On-

132

tario, records that could no longer be stored at the original institution. Patients' files, if they exist, will not likely be accessible. However **registers of admissions** may be open for research and they may disclose about the patient his age, sex, dates of admission and discharge, record of a death or birth, nationality, religious affiliation, residence, disease, attending physician and other information relating to hospital care and fees.

Published records include "Paediatric Admissions to Kingston General Hospital, Kingston, Ontario (1889-1909)" by Dr. Partington in *Families*, Vol. 22, No. 1 (1983) and "Immigrants at Toronto Hospital, 1873" in *Lost in Canada?*, Vol. 11, No. 1 (1983).

The AO finding aid *Records of the Inspector of Asylums, Prisons and Public Charities 1867-1935* includes some records of psychiatric and other hospitals, and facilities for the blind and deaf. Appendix H lists alphabetically the names and dates of estate maintenance files for persons unable to handle their own affairs. Permission for additional information must be sought from the Director, Mental Health Operations Branch, Ministry of Health, Hepburn Block, 8th Floor, Queen's Park, Toronto M7A 1R3.

County Paupers and County Houses of Industry is a pamphlet published in 1894 explaining these charitable institutions and their services. In "The Industrial Home, Newmarket, Ontario" by Norman Jolly in *Families*, Vol. 26, No. 4 (1987) there is some description of the type of people admitted, reports by inspectors and physicians, and rules and regulations. Inmates were needy or homeless people who physically or financially could not exist independently, and Jolly notes that burials at this Home were likely bodies unclaimed by family. In this particular case the physician's annual reports included the very ill and the deaths, which could be a source for a missing ancestor.

INDIAN
RECORDS

In spite of the misnomer, the term Indian has long been used in the classification of records pertaining to native Canadian and Ontario peoples. The Public Records Division of the PAC has published a guide *Records Relating to Indian Affairs (RG 10)* which describes in fifty pages their holdings of the former federal Department of Indian Affairs. The broad categories include Imperial Government administration records 1677-1864, ministerial administration 1786-1970, field office records 1809-1971, agency records 1857-1971 and Indian land records 1680-1956.

A thirty-year restriction applies to these records, but personal or sensitive information is closed, and that includes band membership and enfranchisement files. It is really necessary to consult this guide to determine specific interests, as the records apply to areas throughout the entire country. Much of the collection is available on microfilm, and AO has copies of it. The guide also outlines the history of administration of Indian affairs.

A definitive article by expert David Faux is "Documenting Six Nations Indian Ancestry" in *Families*, Vol. 20, No. 1 (1981). The references and notes at the end of his article make many suggestions for sources for Six Nations ancestry, one of which is Brantford's Museum of the Woodland Indian -- Cultural Educational Centre (Appendix I).

A reference booklet is *A Profile of Native People in Ontario* (see Appendix II), which explores Indian history, status, treaties and locations. Information on Ontario native communities can be located through the Director, Native Communities Branch (Appendix I). See also references to Indian Loyalists in Chapter 11.

TWEEDSMUIR HISTORIES

Women's Institutes, now a world-wide network for rural women, were founded in Ontario. One of their greatest contributions to genealogy, family history and local history is their Tweedsmuir Histories. Each Institute undertook to collect local history information from various sources and to compile it into a continuing history of their particular area. The histories may include interviews with descendants of pioneers, newspaper clippings, family histories, church histories, historical sites, war memorials, photographs and material on any and all social development within the community. Each may be unique in its format and presentation.

Tweedsmuir Histories have been microfilmed for most parts of the province and may be found at AO or local libraries. As nearly all the material is manuscript or hearsay, it is a secondary source for genealogists, but on the other hand may provide anecdotes, information or clues or not available elsewhere.

TELEPHONE DIRECTORIES

A published source of more recent interest are the **Bell Telephone Directories**. Starting before the turn of this century, they do provide a continuity for a name and location. In microfilm form they are available at AO and many libraries, from 1878 to 1979. Of course telephone service began only in the most urban centres, slowly spreading to the rural areas in the twentieth century.

FRATERNAL

Some may question just what a genealogist can learn from fraternal organizations, social or public service groups, but membership alone can add depth of character to an ancestor. If records are available, they might show how an ancestor stood on issues within the group. Two published examples are "Orangeism Takes Root in Ontario" by Dr. Hereward Senior in *Canadian Genealogist*, Vol. 3, No. 1 (1981) and "The Ancient Order of United Workmen" by Helen Schmid in *Families*, Vol. 21, No. 2 (1982). This latter was augmented by "The A.O.U.W. Revisited" in Vol. 22, No. 1 (1983) and "More A.O.U.W. Assessment Notices" in Vol. 26, No. 4 (1987). The assessment notices were for death benefits to kin of members, and give name, age, date and cause of death, name and location of lodge.

A recent publication is *The St. George Society of Toronto: A History and List of Members 1834-1967* by Anne Storey (Appendix II) which also includes burials by the Society in a special burial plot at St. James Cemetery in Toronto.

Some collections held at **AO** with individual finding aids are:

International Order of Oddfellows (IOOF), members 1846-1961
Loyal Orange Lodge, Roxborough Chapter #623, members 1861-1975
Lumbermen's Association, 1887-1908
Preliminary Inventory of Women's Organizations 1926-73
Sons of Temperance, Orono #79, minutebooks 1850-97
Soroptomist International of Toronto, 1933-86
Sudbury and District General Workers Union, Local 902, 1950-68
Toronto Optimist Club, 1923-74

Some representative material at **PAC**:

Canadian Hadassah-WIZO, MG 28, Vol. 74
Imperial Order of Daughters of the Empire (IODE), MG 28, I 198
Royal Canadian Academy of Arts, MG 28, I 126
Toronto Camera Club, MG 28, I 181
Victorian Order of Nurses for Canada, MG 28, I 171
Young Men's Christian Association (YMCA), MG 28, I 198

The annual *Directory of Associations in Canada* may be the most useful guide to finding current names and addresses.

LABOUR
UNIONS

Trade unions or organizations have existed since the nineteenth century, but records for **labour unions** are available mainly as a twentieth century social and economic development. Records from a few unions are at AO but may more are at PAC because of their national nature. The Canadian Labour Congress, which includes its predecessors, deposited its historical records with PAC in 1970. The Congress is an umbrella group of Canadian unions. The largest collections at PAC relate to railway and transportation unions, and most date from the 1940s.

Some of the union records at PAC are: Clothing Workers, Canadian Television and Radio Artists, Canadian Airline Employees, Canadian Union of Public Employees, Knights of Labour, Steelworkers, Textile Workers, Automobile Workers, and many, many others.

ETHNIC

Ethnic groups in Canada were mentioned briefly at the end of Chapter 7. The settling of immigrants from various countries around the globe in Canada over the space of two hundred years has made popular the phrase "Canadian mosaic" in counterpoint to the United States' "melting pot" absorption of immigrants. This is a simplified way of saying that a great majority of immigrants to Canada, many of whom did and still settle in Ontario, retain a strong cultural attachment to their homeland rather than become homogenous Canadians. In many cases this effort to maintain the former customs, language and culture is a direct result of persecution in that former country or displacement during the World Wars.

The Manuscript Division of PAC has established a special **Ethnic Archives** to collect and reflect this cultural diversity. As well, the private papers of many individuals from ethnic communities have been donated for their historic value. Enquiries to PAC or, again, consulting the *Directory of Associations in Canada* should be helpful. Addresses for some groups are given in Appendix I.

Black history in Ontario is being collected and preserved by the North American Black Historical Museum (Appendix I). The story of the "underground railroad" whereby black slaves escaped to Canada is told in Walls' *The Road That Led to Somewhere*. See also "A Proud Past, A Promising Future: Ontario Black

History Society" by Glace Lawrence in *OGS Seminar Annual* (1987). This latter group promotes research and the heritage of black people in Ontario, particularly through education. Some of their projects have included a bibliographic series and a travelling exhibit.

HERALDRY

Heraldry has traditionally been dependent on genealogy as the means to achieve its end, the identification of individuals through heraldic or armorial devices. Canada does not have a heraldic authority to grant coats of arms, but there is some keen interest in the subject and in the establishment of a Canadian authority. Many of the countries which Canadian citizens find roots in have authorities that grant titles and coats of arms, for example the College of Arms in England, and the Court of Lord Lyon in Scotland. Other European countries have also had this function in the past.

To this extent some family historians may come across such a reference, and the appropriate overseas authority must be contacted. Occasionally a legitimate Canadian heir may be sought or found for dormant estates or titles, in which case a genealogy and pedigree will be absolutely necessary for proof of descent.

Current heraldic authorities may be applied to for the personal design and execution of a coat of arms, such as those for municipal corporations and that of the Ontario Genealogical Society.

More pointedly, this section is to warn the novice or unsuspecting that a proper coat of arms is the legal property of the person to whom it has been granted. In Great Britain there are legal strictures to protect such property. A coat of arms is not something decorated with your family surname that you hang above your fireplace. A number of unscrupulous companies have encouraged this practice, to their continuing business (but no other) credit.

A Scottish clan badge may be correctly worn or displayed by anyone of that name as long as it is surrounded by the belt with the clan motto, and is not to be confused with a coat of arms. The clan badge without the belt is properly the crest of the clan chief alone.

There are offshoots of this whole "one big family" scam that call their decorations "family crests" or "family coats of arms", and the ubiquitous family history "books" that condense a surname history and copy pages from telephone directories. The mail solicitation will make it sound as if some unknown individual, usually a woman's name, has at great cost and labour produced a definitive family history for you. Several of these mail order companies have been successfully charged and fined in Canada and the United States for fraudulent advertising,but they simply recur in a near-by location with a new name.

As you become involved in genealogy you may find that relatives and friends will approach you when such a contact has been made with them. It is to your own benefit and credibility that you can tell them unequivo-cally that their own particular family history is quite unique and takes years of dedicated personal research to establish. The old saying, "beware of strangers bearing gifts", applies most aptly.

"Toward the Establishment of A Canadian Heraldic Authority: A Progress Report" by John D. Blackwell in *Families*, Vol. 27, No. 1 (1987) is an up-to-date discus-sion of the situation.

13/Long Distance Research

The "do-it-yourself" genealogist is not totally blocked when a visit to a local Ontario resource centre is not possible for personal examination of records material. The public library in your home town may have more than you think. You might ask if they can acquire some of the more general publications. A university library, if accessible, collects historical material relevant to the courses it offers. A local genealogical or historical society may be on a subscription exchange with OGS; again, you might enquire if this is a feasible request.

CORRESPONDENCE

Writing letters is the genealogist's lot when records are not accessible. Remember that American stamps or those of other countries can not be used in Canada. If you are not Canadian, ask your local genealogical society how to obtain Canadian stamps. Genealogical societies with international members usually have people who will purchase stamps of their own country for other members. Otherwise two **International Postal Reply Coupons** should be sent with every letter, and always a self-adressed envelope. This enclosure can speed up response and establish an important sense of good will.

Requesting a search from the register of a local church, a place that doesn't employ staff for this purpose, is better received if a token money order is enclosed. Minimum enclosure should be $5, and definitely more should be sent depending on how much work you are asking for. A personal suggestion is to offer the money as payment to the person who searches the registers; if the volunteer searcher should refuse the money, it can be directed to the church itself as a donation.

Unfortunately there will always be a small percentage who will not reply no matter how nice or how desperate you sound. Always be concise and as brief as possible.

Writing to a church archives should obtain for you the address of an individual church, if you supplied a placename. You may or may not be told that the registers you seek are in their holdings, according to their policy and staff time. For instance, the PCA (see Appendix I for addresses) will try to accommodate written requests from such a distance that precludes a personal visit. The UCA can't do this, but will send a list of professional researchers.

Both the PAC and AO will answer limited queries but we urge that you not abuse the system. Cutbacks in government spending and staff in these public institutions could possibly reduce this service. The PAC will supply a list of local researchers familiar with their holdings, but AO may only suggest contacting the Ontario Genealogical Society.

We have suggested many types of directories that supply addresses for various institutions, through the chapters of this book. Current city directories and the Yellow Pages of a telephone directory are other means of obtaining individual church addresses, and these are normally available at a large public library for all areas of the province.

INTER LIBRARY LOAN (ILL)

Many records that have been microfilmed are available through Inter Library Loan anywhere in the U.S. or Canada from the PAC. The requirement is that your local library belong to the system and have a microfilm reader. Films are loaned to a library (**not to an individual!**) for a small charge to cover postage.

So the good news is that just about everything at **PAC** mentioned in this text as "microfilmed" can be read by you in your home town library. You may have to write PAC first to obtain the film numbers, such as those for census or church registers,for ordering at your library. This may not be necessary if you describe the material in detail with dates and placenames.

The bad news is that **AO** does not participate in Inter Library Loan. Records unique to AO are presently available only on site. There are some plans to change this and join the ILL system, but this will be dependent on future budgets and staffing.

You will find that most smaller local libraries, museums and archives will generally respond to a written query, although many have only part-time hours and staff. You can save yourself time and frustration by telephoning in advance of a visit; some museums and archives may only be open seasonally.

LDS LIBRARY

Another library is that of the Church of Jesus Christ of Latter Day Saints, more popularly known as Mormons, long called the LDS Library among genealogists. It is a requirement of their faith that Mormons trace their ancestry, and by collecting copies of genealogical records from all over the world, the LDS Church has made it easier for members to do this. The main LDS Library in Salt Lake City, now called the **Family History Library**, contains the world's largest collection of genealogical records. Of course these are not all "Mormon" records; Mormon ancestry goes beyond its relatively recent beginnings to roots in other countries and religions.

Microfilm copies of anything in their holdings can be sent to one of their branch libraries from Salt Lake City for a small loan and postage charge. Non-LDS church members are welcome to use the facilities of a branch library or the main Family History Library. The staff at the branch libraries are volunteer church members who will help you to use appropriate catalogues and finding aids for ordering microfilm, but it is not part of their job to undertake research. Not every LDS church has a branch library. However in Ontario (Appendix I) and throughout North America, they are found in most major communities. Telephone calls should be made first to determine their part-time hours.

Their holdings for Ontario are growing all the time, and include deeds, indexes to deeds, abstract indexes, the Ontario Land Records index, some Surrogate Court indexes, some collectors' and assessment rolls, and a variety of church registers. As mentioned in Chapter 3, they have microfilm copies of most Ontario Catholic churches. A filming crew has been working at AO for some time and this will make accessible much more of the AO material.

Dawn Broughton's "LDS Branch Genealogical Libraries in Ontario" in *Families*, Vol. 25, No. 4 (1986) explores their research aids with illustrations and gives information on various locations and open hours. David Pratt wrote "Using the IGI to Solve Research Problems" in *Families*, Vol. 20, No. 4 (1981).

HIRED RESEARCHERS

There is no accreditation or degree-granting system in Ontario that examines and judges the credentials of professional genealogical researchers. Nor is there a country-wide such system in Canada. But there is a growing number of resident Ontario genealogists who are experienced in the records of major institutions and of smaller local collections, who advertise in publications like *Families* and *Canadian Genealogist*. Classified ads in those magazines are one way to obtain names. The best advice in this case is to query two or more to satisfy your own judgment from written responses and to reach an agreement with one of them. Fees will vary, and may range from hourly rates to specific search charges.

If you receive a list of professional researchers from some institution or resource centre, it normally will not recommend one particular person. They cannot be responsible for the calibre of an independent researcher.

See "Wanted: Hired Genealogist" in *Canadian Genealogist*, Vol. 4, No. 1 (1982) by Brenda Merriman for additional tips on what to expect from, and what to provide to a professional.

Until a Canada-wide federation of genealogical societies undertakes to establish an examination and accreditation system similar to the operating Genealogical Institute of the Maritimes (Nova Scotia, New Brunswick,Prince Edward Island), some researchers in other parts of Canada, including Ontario, have contented themselves with the challenge of meeting internationally accepted standards set by the Board for Certification (P.O. Box 19165, Washington, DC 20034, U.S.A.). Two of their several categories are Certified Genealogist (CG) and Certified Genealogical Record Searcher (CGRS). A second system that applies to North America is the Accredited Genealogists' (AG) Program (c/o Genealogical Society of Utah, 35 N. West Temple, Salt Lake City, UT 84150, U.S.A.). Both these groups will supply an enquirer with a list of their successful candidates when a stamped, self-addressed long envelope is provided.

Another useful article appeared in *OGS Seminar Annual* (1985) called "A Workshop with Professional Genealogists".

QUERIES

Inserting queries in OGS *Families* and other genealogical magazines is a way to contact others for mutual research interests. The section in *Families* is called "The Name Game" and you must be a member of the Society to take advantage of the service. In fifty words or less you can state your genealogical problem or basic ancestral data, subject to editing and abbreviation by the Queries Editor. It takes some consideration to evaluate and compress your information and to state clearly what you are seeking. Samples can be seen in every issue of *Families* and *Canadian Genealogist*.

When a contact is made, it often saves "dead-end" frustration, research time expended in the wrong direction and duplication of effort. Offers on your part to exchange information and replies to all letters are basic courtesy. Joining an OGS Branch can open up new doors to source material.

"I cannot but condemn the carelessness, not to say ingratitude, of those ... who can give no better account of the place where their fathers and grand-fathers were born, than the child unborn .... I could almost wish that a moderate fine were imposed on such heirs, whose fathers were born before them, and yet they know not where they were born."

Thomas Fuller,
The Worthies of England 1662

Appendix I: RESOURCE CENTRES

A) Major Repositories and Resource Centres

PAC

National Archives of Canada
395 Wellington Street
Ottawa, Ontario K1A 0N3
(...Manuscript Division
...Government Archives Division)

AO

Archives of Ontario
77 Grenville Street
Toronto, Ontario M7A 2R9

RGO

Office of the Registrar General
MacDonald Block
Queen's Park
Toronto, Ontario M7A 1Y5

OGS Library
Canadiana Collection, North York Library
North York Centre, 6th Floor
North York, Ontario M2N 5N9

Metropolitan Toronto Central Library
789 Yonge Street
Toronto, Ontario M4W 2G8

National Library of Canada
395 Wellington Street
Ottawa, Ontario K1A 0N4

Official Documents Section   (Copies of Patents)
Ministry of Government Services
Hearst Block, 3rd Floor
Queen's Park
Toronto, Ontario M7A 1N3

Ministry of Natural Resources   (Current Patent
Land Management Branch   Index)
Titles Section, Room 6621
Whitney Block
Queen's Park
Toronto, Ontario M7A 1W3

Query Response Centre   (Records of Entry)
Employment and Immigration Canada
10th Floor
Place du Portage, Phase IV
Hull, Quebec K1A 0J9

Records Control
Citizenship Registration Branch
Secretary of State
P.O. Box 7000
Sydney, Nova Scotia B1P 6G5

Adoption Disclosure Register
700 Bay Street, 2nd Floor
Toronto, Ontario M7A 1E9

Royal Canadian Military Institute
426 University Avenue
Toronto, Ontario M5G 1S9

Legislative Library of Ontario
Parliament Buildings
Queen's Park
Toronto, Ontario M7A 1A2

Director, Native Community Branch
Ministry of Citizenship and Culture
5th Floor, 77 Bloor Street West
Toronto, Ontario M7A 2R9

HBC   Hudson's Bay Company Archives
Provincial Archives of Manitoba
200 Vaughan Street
Winnipeg, Manitoba R3C 1T5

Children's Aid Societies
Children's and Adults' Services
Ministry of Community and Social Services
Hepburn Block, 6th Floor
Queen's Park
Toronto, Ontario M7A 1E9

Supreme Court of Ontario
130 Queen Street W.
Toronto, Ontario M5H 2N5

Office of the Surrogate Clerk   (Post-1976 indexes)
Phoenix House
439 University Avenue, 3rd Floor
Toronto, Ontario M5G 1Y8

UCA   United Church of Canada Archives
Victoria University
73 Queen's Park Crescent East
Toronto, Ontario M5S 1K7

PCA   Presbyterian Church in Canada Archives
Knox College
59 St. George Street
Toronto, Ontario M5S 2E6

CBA

Canadian Baptist Archives
McMaster Divinity College
McMaster University
Hamilton, Ontario L8S 4K1

Canadian Jewish Congress
Ontario Region Archives
4600 Bathurst
Willowdale, Ontario M2R 3V2

Mennonite Archives of Ontario
Conrad Grebel College
University of Waterloo
Waterloo, Ontario N2L 3G1

Lutheran Church in America
Eastern Canada Synod Archives
Wilfrid Laurier University
Waterloo, Ontario N2L 3C5

Canadian Society of Friends (Quaker)
60 Lowther Avenue
Toronto, Ontario M5R 1C7

George Scott Railton Heritage Centre Archives
Salvation Army
2130 Bayview Avenue
Toronto, Ontario M4N 3K6

Canadian Disciples Archives
39 Arkell Road
R.R. #2
Guelph, Ontario N1H 6H8

Museum of the Woodland Indian
Cultural Educational Centre
184 Mohawk Street
Brantford, Ontario N3S 2X2

Ontario Association of Cemeteries
1723 Elgin Mills Road East
R.R. #2
Gormley, Ontario L0H 1G0

Wellington County Archives
R.R. #1
Fergus, Ontario N1M 2W3

Belleville Public Library
223 Pinncale St.
Belleville, Ontario K8N 3A7

Guelph Public Library
100 Norfolk St.
Guelph, Ontario N1H 4J6

Anglican Church of Canada:

Diocese of Algoma
530 Queen St. E., Box 637
Sault Ste. Marie, Ontario P6A 5N7

Diocese of Huron
Huron Church House
Box 308
London, Ontario N6A 4W3

Diocese of Keewatin
Box 118
Kenora, Ontario P9N 3X1

Diocese of Moosonee
Box 841
Schumaker, Ontario P0N 1G0

Diocese of Niagara
67 Victoria Avenue S.
Hamilton, Ontario L8N 2S8

Diocese of Ontario
90 Johnson Street
Kingston, Ontario K7L 1X7

Diocese of Ottawa
71 Bronson Avenue
Ottawa, Ontario K1R 6G6

Diocese of Toronto
135 Adelaide Street E.
Toronto, Ontario M5C 1L8

Roman Catholic Church:

Archdiocese of Kingston, Archives
279 Johnson Street
Kingston, Ontario K7L 4X8

Archdiocese of Ottawa, Archives
256 King Edward Avenue
Ottawa, Ontario K1N 7M1

Archdiocese of Toronto, Archives
355 Church Street
Toronto, Ontario M5B 1Z8

Diocese of Alexandria-Cornwall
Box 1388
Cornwall, Ontario K6H 5V4

Diocese of Hamilton
714 King Street W.
Hamilton, Ontario L8P 1C7

Diocese of Hearst
Box 817
Hearst, Ontario P0L 1N0

Diocese of London
1070 Waterloo Street
London, Ontario N6A 3Y2

Diocese of Moosonee
Box 40
Moosonee, Ontario P0L 1Y0

Diocese of Pembroke
Box 7
Pembroke, Ontario K8A 6X1

Diocese of Peterborough
Box 175
Peterborough, Ontario K9J 6Y4

Diocese of St. Catharines
3 Lyman Street
St. Catharines, Ontario L2R 5M8

Diocese of Sault Ste. Marie
480 McIntyre Street W.
North Bay, Ontario P1B 2Z4

Diocese of Thunder Bay
213 Archibald Street S.
Thunder Bay, Ontario P7E 1G4

LDS   *Church of Jesus Christ of Latter Day Saints, Libraries:*

35 N. West Temple
Salt Lake City, UT 84150, U.S.A.

95 Melbert Avenue
Etobicoke, Ontario M9C 4V3

701 Stone Church Road E.
Hamilton, Ontario L8W 1A9

Glenburnie, Ontario K0H 1S0

10 Lorrain Avenue
Kitchener, Ontario N2B 2M8

1139 Riverside Drive
London, Ontario N6H 2T7

SW corner Thornton Road N. & Rossland Road W.
Oshawa, Ontario

1017 Prince of Wales Drive
Ottawa, Ontario K2C 3K1

1400 Murphy Road N.
Sarnia, Ontario N7S 5P6

2255 Ponderosa Drive
R.R. #1
Thunder Bay, Ontario P7C 4T9

500 Toke Street
Timmins, Ontario P4N 6W1

351 Glenridge
St. Catharines, Ontario L2T 3K6

Major University Libraries with regional collections:

Brock University
St. Catharines, Ontario L2S 3A1

Mills Memorial Library
McMaster University
1280 Main Street W.
Hamilton, Ontario L8S 4L6

Queen's University
Kingston, Ontario K7L 3N6

McLaughlin Library
University of Guelph
Guelph, Ontario N1G 2W1

University of Toronto
Thomas Fisher Library
120 St. George Street, 4th Floor
Toronto, Ontario M5S 1A5

John P. Robarts Research Library
University of Toronto
130 St. George Street
Toronto, Ontario M5S 1A5

D.B. Weldon Library
University of Western Ontario
London, Ontario N6A 3K7

B) Associations, many with periodicals and publications

Ontario Genealogical Society
40 Orchard View Boulevard
Suite 253
Toronto, Ontario M4R 1B9

United Empire Loyalists' Association of Canada
Dominion Headquarters
23 Prince Arthur Avenue
Toronto, Ontario M5R 1B2

Ontario Historical Society
5151 Yonge Street
North York, Ontario M2N 5P5

Pennsylvania German Folklore Society of Canada
c/o Mrs. Lorna Bergey
R.R. #2
New Hamburg, Ontario N0B 2G0

Huguenot Society of Canada
10 Adelaide St. E.
Toronto, Ontario M5C 1H5

The Heraldry Society of Canada
P.O. Box 697, Station B
Ottawa, Ontario K1P 5P8

The Multicultural History Society of Ontario
43 Queen's Park Crescent E.
Toronto, Ontario M5S 2C3

Northwest Territory Canadian and French Heritage
Center
P.O. Box 26372
St. Louis Park, MN 55426, U.S.A.

Ontario Black History Society
352 Sheppard Avenue E.
Willowdale, Ontario M2N 3B4

North American Black Historical Museum and Cultural
Centre
277 King Street, P.O. Box 12
Amherstburg, Ontario N9V 2C7

Norfolk Historical Society
Eva Brook Donly Museum
109 Norfolk Street S.
Simcoe, Ontario N3Y 2W3

Société franco-ontarienne d'histoire et de généalogie
C.P. 720, Succ. B
Ottawa, Ontario K1P 5P8

The Glengarry Genealogical Society
R.R. #1
Lancaster, Ontario K0C 1N0

Lanark County Genealogical Society
c/o Robert Allan
53 Wilson Street W.
Perth, Ontario K7H 2N3

Nor-West Historical and Genealogical Society
P.O. Box 124
Vermilion Bay, Ontario P0V 2V0

Canadian Society of Mayflower Descendants
c/o Miss D. Clarke
38 Dennett Drive
Agincourt, Ontario M1S 2E7

Stormont, Dundas and Glengarry Genealogical Society
c/o Sandra McMillan
618 Pescod Avenue
Cornwall, Ontario K6J 2J5

Geraldton Genealogical and Historical Society
P.O. Box 801
Geraldton, Ontario P0T 1M0

Muskoka-Parry Sound Genealogical Group
R.R. #4, Bella Lake
Huntsville, Ontario P0A 1K0

The Society of Loyalist Descendants
c/o Joe McLaurin
P.O. Box 848
Rockingham, NC 28379, U.S.A.

Jewish Genealogical Society of Toronto
c/o B'nai Brith House
15 Hove Street
Downsview, Ontario M3H 4Y8

Société de Généalogie de l'Outaouais Inc.
C.P. 2025, Succ. B
Hull, Quebec J8X 3Z2

Waterdown - E. Flamborough Heritage Society
Box 1044
Waterdown, Ontario L0R 2H0

Appendix II: PUBLICATIONS

A) Publishers and Book Sellers
(ask for lists/catalogues)

Ontario Genealogical Society
40 Orchard View Boulevard
Suite 253
Toronto, Ontario M4R 1B9

Generation Press (*Canadian Genealogist* and others)
172 King Henrys Boulevard
Agincourt, Ontario M1T 2V6

Wheatfield Press
Box 205, St. James Postal Station
Winnipeg, Manitoba R3J 3R4

Lost in Canada? (Serial Publication)
Joy Reisinger, Editor
1020 Central
Sparta, WI 54656, U.S.A.

Mika Publishing Company
P.O. Box 536
Belleville, Ontario K8N 5B2

Dundurn Press Limited
P.O. Box 245, Station F
Toronto, Ontario M4Y 2L5

Hunterdon House (*The Ontario Register* and others)
38 Swan Street
Lambertville, NJ 08530, U.S.A.

The Bookcellar
144 James Street South
Hamilton, Ontario L8P 3A2

The Highway Book Shop
Cobalt, Ontario P0J 1C0

Government Publication Centre (PAC Publications)
Supply and Services Canada
Ottawa, Ontario K1A 0S9

Ontario Government Bookstore
880 Bay Street
Toronto, Ontario M7A 1N8
(out-of-town customers write to:
Publications Services Section, 5th Floor, as above)

153

Cumming Publishers (County Atlases)
Box 23
Stratford, Ontario N5A 6S8

Huronia-Canadiana Books
Box 685
Alliston, Ontario L0M 1A0

Traces
1024 Motherwell Road NE
Calgary, Alberta T2E 6E7

Highland Heritage
R.R. #1
Lancaster, Ontario K0C 1N0

Bur-Mor Publications
359 West Gore Street
Stratford, Ontario N5A 1K9

Mildred Livingston
St. Lawrence Court
R.R. #1
Prescott, Ontario K0E 1T0

Allen E. Jewitt, Sr., Publisher
4011 Monroe Avenue
Hamburg, NY 14075, U.S.A.

Walrus Press
420 Victoria St.
Kingston, Ontario K7L 3Z5

B) Maps and Supplies

Ontario Genealogical Society
40 Orchard View Boulevard
Suite 253
Toronto, Ontario M4R 1B9

Ministry of Transportation & Communications
1201 Wilson Avenue
Downsview, Ontario M3M 1J8

Perly's Variprint Limited
1050 Eglinton Avenue West
Toronto, Ontario M6C 2C5

Generation Press
172 King Henrys Boulevard
Agincourt, Ontario M1T 2V6

Cluny Press
Box 2207
Kingston, Ontario K7L 5J9

The Bloomfield Line
c/o Gordon Crouse
Box 212
Bloomfield, Ontario K0K 1G0

C) SELECTED IMPORTANT BOOKS: General Interest

A Profile of Native People in Ontario. Toronto: Ministry of Citizenship and Culture, 1983.

Aitken, Barbara, Dawn Broughton, and Yvonne Crouch, *Some Ontario References and Sources for the Family Historian.* Toronto: OGS, 1984.

Allen, Robert S., *Loyalist Literature, An Annotated Bibliographic Guide to the Writings on the Loyalists of the American Revolution.* Toronto: Dundurn Press, 1982.

Anderek, Paul A., and Richard A. Pence, *Computer Genealogy.* Salt Lake City, UT: Ancestry Incorporated, 1985.

Antliff, W. Bruce, *Loyalist Settlements, 1783-1789, New Evidence of Canadian Claims.* Toronto: Ministry of Citizenship and Culture, 1985.

Baxter, Angus, *In Search of Your Roots.* Toronto: Macmillan Company, 1978.

Beddoe, Lt. Cdr. Alan, *Beddoe's Canadian Heraldry.* Rev. by Col. Strome Galloway. Belleville: Mika Publishing, no date.

Brown, Wallace, *The King's Friends, the Composition and Nature of the American Loyalist Claimants.* Providence, RI: Brown University Press, 1965.

Bruce, R. M., *The Loyalist Trail.* Kingston: Jackson Press, 1965.

Bureau of Archives, Second Report. Toronto: Province of Ontario, 1904. Reprint in microfiche, AO 1985.

Canadian Almanac and Directory. Toronto: Copp Clark, annual.

Carter, Floreen Ellen, *Place Names of Ontario.* London: Phelps Publishing, 1985.

Catalogue of Census Returns on Microfilm 1666-1891. Ottawa: PAC, 1987.

Chadwick, Edward M., *Ontario Families: Genealogies of United Empire Loyalist and Other Pioneer Families of Upper Canada.* (1894) Reprint Belleville: Mika Publishing, 1972.

Checklist of Parish Registers. Ottawa: PAC, 1986.

Coderre, John, *Searching in the Public Archives.* Ottawa: Ottawa Branch OGS, 1972.

Coldham, Peter W., *American Loyalist Claims, Vol. I.* Washington, DC: National Genealogical Society, 1980.

County Paupers and County Houses of Industry. Toronto: Prisoners' Aid Association of Canada, 1894.

Court of Probate: Registers and Estate Files at the Archives of Ontario (1793-1859). Toronto: OGS, 1986.

Craig, Gerald, *Upper Canada: The Formative Years, 1784-1841.* Toronto: McClelland and Stewart, 1963.

Crowder, Norman K., *Indexes to Ontario Census Records.* Toronto: OGS, 1987.

Dictionary of Canadian Biography. Vols. I-VI (1000-1835), VIII-XI (1851-90). Toronto: University of Toronto Press, 1966-87.

Directory of Associations in Canada, General editor, Brian Land. Toronto: University of Toronto Press, 1973-.

Directory of Canadian Archives. Ottawa: Bureau of Canadian Archivists and Association of Canadian Archivists, 1981.

Directory of Member Cemeteries. Gormley, Ontario: Ontario Association of Cemeteries, 1983.

Directory of Ontario Public Libraries. Toronto: Provincial Library Service, Ontario Ministry of Culture and Recreation, 1979.

Directory of the Province of Ontario, 1857. Lambertville, NJ: Hunterdon House, 1987.

Directory of Surnames, Special Edition (and annually). Toronto: OGS, 1987.

Doane, Gilbert, *Searching For Your Ancestors.* New York: Bantam Books, 1974.

Egerton, Hugh E., *The Royal Commission on the Losses and Services of American Loyalists, 1783-1785.* New York: Burt Franklin & Co., 1971. Reprint of 1915 edition.

Elliott, Bruce S., *Irish Migrants in the Canadas*. Kingston: Queen's-McGill Press, 1987.

Filby, P. William, with Mary K. Meyer, *Passenger and Immigration Lists Index: a guide to published arrival records of about 500,000 passengers who came to the United States and Canada in the seventeenth, eighteenth and nineteenth centuries*. Detroit: Gale Research, 1981. Several supplements.

Filby, P. William, *Directory of Libraries with Local History/Genealogy Collections*. Wilmington, DE: Scholarly Resources, 1988.

Fryer, Mary B., *King's Men, The Soldier Founders of Ontario*. Toronto: Dundurn Press, 1980.

Fryer, Mary B., and Lt. Col. William A. Smy, *Rolls of the Provincial (Loyalist) Corps, Canadian Command, American Revolutionary Period*. Toronto: Dundurn Press, 1981.

Gates, Lillian F., *Land Policies of Upper Canada*. Toronto: University of Toronto Press, 1968.

Gilchrist, J. Brian, compiler and editor, *The Inventory of Ontario Newspapers 1793-1986*. Toronto: Micromedia Limited, 1987.

Genealogical Sources, Archives of Ontario. Toronto: AO, 1981.

General Guide Series. Ottawa: PAC. Guides have been published for all Divisions of the National Archives, available from the Government Publications Centre as above in Section A.

Grenville, John H., *Searching For a Soldier in the British Army or Canadian Militia*. Kingston Branch OGS, 1977.

Harland, Derek, *Genealogical Research Standards*. Salt Lake City: Bookcraft, 1963.

Inventory of Cemeteries in Ontario, A Genealogical Research Guide. Toronto: OGS, 1987.

Jonasson, Eric, *The Canadian Genealogical Handbook*. Winnipeg: Wheatfield Press, 1978.

Jonasson, Eric, *Canadian Veterans of the War of 1812*. Winnipeg: Wheatfield Press, 1981.

Jonasson, Eric, *Untangling the Tree: Organizational Systems for the Family Historian*. Winnipeg: Wheatfield Press, 1983.

Jones, James E., *Pioneer Crimes and Punishments in Toronto and the Home District*. Toronto: George N. Morang, 1924.

Journals of Proceedings of the House of Assembly of Upper Canada, 1792-1840, (published in *Bureau of Archives Reports Nos. 6, 8, 9, 10, 11*); Microfilmed 1825-40.

Journals of the Legislative Assembly of the Province of Canada, 1841-1867. Microfilmed.

Kennedy, Patricia, *How to Trace Your Loyalist Ancestors*. Ottawa: Ottawa Branch OGS, 1972.

Kennedy, Patricia, and Janine Roy, *Tracing Your Ancestors in Canada*. Ottawa: PAC, 1983.

Kieran, Sheila, *The Family Matters: Two Centuries of Family Law and Life in Ontario*. Toronto: Key Porter Books, 1986.

Lackey, Richard S., *Cite Your Sources*. New Orleans: Polyanthos, 1980.

Loyalist Lineages of Canada 1783-1983. Toronto: Toronto Branch, United Empire Loyalist Association, 1984.

Magee, Joan, *Loyalist Mosaic: A Multi-Ethnic Heritage*. Toronto: Dundurn Press, 1984.

Mathews, Hazel C., *The Mark of Honour*. Toronto: University of Toronto Press, 1965.

McFall, David and Jean, *Land Records in Ontario Registry Offices*. Toronto: OGS, 1984.

McKenzie, Donald A., *Death Notices from the* Christian Guardian *1836-1850*. Lambertville, NJ: Hunterdon House, 1982.

McKenzie, Donald A., *Death Notices from the* Christian Guardian *1851-1860*. Lambertville, NJ: Hunterdon House, 1984.

McKenzie, Donald A., *More Notices from Methodist Newspapers 1830-1857*. Lambertville, NJ: Hunterdon House, 1986.

Mennie-de Varennes, Kathleen, *Annotated Bibliography of Genealogical Works in Canada*, Vol. 1. Ottawa: National Library of Canada and Fitzhenry and Whiteside, 1986.

Mika, Nick and Helma, *Places in Ontario, Their Names, Origins, and History. Part 1, A-E; Part 2, F-M; Part 3, N-Z.* Belleville: Mika Publishing, 1977, 1981, 1983.

Morton, Desmond, *A Military History of Canada*. Edmonton: Hurtig Publishers, 1985.

Municipal Directory (annual). Toronto: Ontario Ministry of Municipal Affairs.

Old U.E. List. Baltimore, MD: Genealogical Publishing Company, 1984. Reprint of 1885 edition.

Ontario Historic Sites, Museums, Galleries and Plaques. Toronto: Ministry of Culture and Recreation, Heritage Conservation Division.

People of Ontario, 1600-1900, Noel M. Elliot, editor. London: Genealogical Research Library, c1984.

Reid, William D., *Death Notices of Ontario*. Lambertville, NJ: Hunterdon House, 1980.

Reid, William D., *The Loyalists in Ontario, The Sons and Daughters of American Loyalists of Upper Canada.* Lambertville, NJ: Hunterdon House, 1973.

Reid, William D., *Marriage Notices of Ontario*. Lambertville, NJ: Hunterdon House, 1980.

Rubincam, Milton, editor, *Genealogical Research: Methods and Sources, Vol. I.* Washington, DC: American Society of Genealogists, 1980.

Ryder, Dorothy E., *Checklist of Canadian Directories, 1790-1850.* Ottawa: National Library of Canada, 1979.

Sabine, Lorenzo, *Loyalists of the American Revolution.* Baltimore, MD: Genealogical Publishing Company, 1979. Reprint.

Schweitzer, George K., *Civil War Genealogy.* Knoxville, TN: George K. Schweitzer, 1984.

Schweitzer, George K., *Revolutionary War Genealogy.* Knoxville, TN: George K. Schweitzer, 1984.

Schweitzer, George K., *War of 1812 Genealogy.* Knoxville, TN: George K. Schweitzer, 1983.

Shepard, Catherine, *Surrogate Court Records at the Archives of Ontario.* Toronto: OGS, 1984.

Smith, W.H., *Canadian Gazetteer.* Toronto: Coles Publishing Company, 1972. Reprint of 1846 edition.

Stevenson, Noel C., *Genealogical Evidence.* Laguna Hills, CA: Aegean Park Press, 1979.

Stevenson, Noel C., *Search and Research: The Researcher's Handbook.* Salt Lake City: Deseret Book Co., 1964.

Union List of Manuscripts in Canadian Repositories. Ottawa: PAC, 1975. (Annual supplements)

Whyte, Donald, *A Dictionary of Scottish Emigrants to Canada Before Confederation.* Toronto: OGS, 1986.

Wilson, Don, compiler, *Readings in Ontario Genealogical Sources.* Toronto: Conference on Ontario Genealogical Sources, 1979.

Wilson, Thomas B., *Marriage Bonds of Ontario 1803-1834.* Lambertville, NJ: Hunterdon House, 1985.

Wilson, Thomas B., *Ontario Marriage Notices*. Lambertville, NJ: Hunterdon House, 1982.

Wright, Norman E., and David Pratt, *Genealogical Research Essentials*. Salt Lake City: Bookcraft Inc., 1967.

D) SELECTED IMPORTANT BOOKS: Local Research Aids

Aitken, Barbara B., *Local Histories of Ontario Municipalities, 1951-1977: A Bibliography*. Toronto: Ontario Library Association, 1978.

Aitken, Barbara B., and H. Dawn Broughton, *Tracing Your Ancestors in Frontenac and Lennox and Addington Counties*. Kingston: Kingston Branch OGS, 1987.

Anderson, Allan J., *Diocese of Ontario (Anglican Church of Canada) Archives: Preliminary Inventory, 1980*. Kingston: Anglican Diocese of Ontario, 1980.

Bagnall, Kenneth, *The Little Immigrants*. Toronto: Macmillan of Canada, 1980.

Bertrand, J.P., *Highway of Destiny*. [Thunder Bay District] New York: Vantage Press, 1959.

Blackburn,Helen, and Diane French, Judith Mitton, Jean Zimmer, Carol Marcelle, *Tracing Your Family in Kent County, A Guide for Beginners and Experts*. Chatham: Kent County Branch OGS, n.d.

Bonk, Darryl, *How to Trace Your Family in Oxford County*. Oxford County Branch OGS, 1981.

Boyce, Gerald E., *Historic Hastings*. Belleville: Hastings County Council, 1967.

Canniff, William, *The Settlement of Upper Canada, with Specific Reference to the Bay of Quinte*. Belleville: Mika Publishing, 1971. Reprint of 1869 edition.

Coffman, Barbara, *Samuel Fry the Weaver and the Mennonites of the Twenty*. Vol. 8, Pennsylvania German Folklore Society of Ontario, 1982.

Coleman, Thelma, *The Canada Company*. Stratford: County of Perth, Perth County Historical Board, and Cumming Publishers, 1978.

Coombe, Geraldine, *Muskoka: Past and Present*. Toronto: McGraw-Hill Ryerson, c 1976.

County Marriage Registers of Ontario, Canada, 1858-1869, Vols. 1-17. [Indexes] Agincourt: Generation Press.

DeMarce, Virginia, *German Military Settlers in Canada, After the American Revolution*. Sparta, WI: Joy Reisinger, 1984.

Dorian, Charles, *The First 75 Years; A Headline History of Sudbury, Canada*. Devon, England: A.H. Stockwell, 1959.

Dorland, Arthur G., *The Quakers in Canada*. Toronto: Canadian Friends Historical Association, 1968.

Drury, Ernest C., *All for a Beaver Hat; a History of Early Simcoe County*. Toronto: Ryerson Press, 1959.

Eby, Ezra E., *A Biographical History of Early Settlers and their Descendants in Waterloo Township*. Revised 1971 by Eldon D. Weber with an index, maps and documents.

1837 Directory for the City of Toronto and the Home District. Toronto: Toronto Branch OGS, 1987. Reprint of 1837 edition.

Elford, Jean T., *History of Lambton County*. Sarnia: Lambton County Historical Society, 1969.

Elliott, Bruce S., *Tracing Your Ottawa Family*. Ottawa: Corporation of the City of Ottawa, 1980, revised 1984.

Epp, Frank, *Mennonites in Canada 1786-1920: The History of a Separate People*. Toronto: Macmillan, 1969.

Ermatinger, Edward, *Life of Colonel Talbot and the Talbot Settlement*. Belleville: Mika Publishing, 1972. Reprint of 1859 edition.

Files, Angela, *Tracing Your Family in Brant County.* Mercantile Press, n.d.

Files, Angela, and Gary Sheldrick, *Church Directory for the County of Brant.* Brantford: Brant County OGS, 1985.

From Stone ... To Steel: An Historical Guide to People, Events and Places in Middlesex County. London: Middlesex County Board of Education, 1975.

Gillespie, Jack, *A Guide to Educational Records in Possession of County Boards of Education in Eastern Ontario.* Toronto: Ontario Institute for Studies in Education, 1972.

Guide to Sources for the Study of Canadian Jewry. Ottawa: PAC, 1978.

Harkness, John G., *Stormont, Dundas and Glengarry, A History, 1784-1945.* Ottawa: Mutual Press, 1972. Reprint of 1946 edition.

Harrison, Phyllis, *The Home Children: Their Personal Stories.* Winnipeg: Watson & Dwyer Publishing, c1979.

Herrington, Walter S., *History of the County of Lennox and Addington.* Belleville: Mika Publishing, 1972. Reprint of 1913 edition.

History of the County of Welland. Belleville: Mika Publishing, 1972. Reprint of 1887 edition.

History of the Great Lakes. Cleveland: Freshwater Press, 1972. Reprint of 1899 edition.

Hodgins, John George, *Documentary History of Education in Upper Canada.* Toronto: Warwick Bros. & Rutter, 1894-1910.

Jewitt, Allen E., *Early Canadian Marriages in Erie County, New York, 1840-1875.* Hamburg, NY: Allen E. Jewitt, 1982.

Johnson, Charles M., *The Head of the Lake: A History of Wentworth County.* Hamilton: Wentworth County Council, 1958.

Johnson, Leo A., *History of the County of Ontario, 1615-1875.* Whitby: Corporation of the County of Ontario, 1973.

Johnston, Walter S., and Hugh J. Johnston, *History of Perth County to 1967.* Stratford: County of Perth, 1967.

Kennedy, Clyde C., *The Upper Ottawa Valley.* Pembroke: Renfrew County Council, 1970.

Ker, Robert, *St. George's Parish Church, St. Catharines.* St. Catharines: Star Print, 1891.

Kirby, William, *Annals of Niagara.* Belleville: Mika Publishing, 1972. Reprint of 1896 edition.

Leavitt, Thaddeus, *History of Leeds and Grenville.* Belleville: Mika Publishing, 1975. Reprint of 1879 edition.

Leitch, Adelaide, *Into the High County; The Story of Dufferin.* Orangeville: Corporation of the County of Dufferin, c1975.

Mann, Trudy, and Jan Speers, *People of Peel, Indexes to Genealogical Source Material. Mississauga*: Mann & Speers, 1981.

Matthews, Hazel C., *Frontier Spies, the British Secret Service, Northern Department, During the Revolutionary War.* Fort Meyers: Ace Press, 1971.

McGill, Jean S., *A Pioneer History of the County of Lanark.* Bewdley: Clay Publishing Co., 1968.

Morland, William F., *Ontario and the Canadian North, Vol. 3: Canadian Local Histories to 1950: A Bibliography.* Toronto: University of Toronto Press, 1978.

Nelles, Robert B., *County of Haldimand in the Days of Auld Lang Syne.* Toronto: Canadian House, c 1970. Reprint of 1905 edition.

O'Gallagher, M., *Grosse Ile Gateway to Canada 1832-1937.* Quebec: Carraig Books, 1984.

Ontario's Heritage, A Guide to Archival Resources, Vol. 1 (Peterborough Region), Vol. 7 (Peel Region), Vol. 12 (North-East Ontario). Cheltenham: Boston Mills

Press, 1978-80; Vol. 4 (Kingston and Frontenac County), Toronto: TAAG Education Foundation, 1986.

Owen, E.A., *Pioneer Sketches of Long Point Settlement*. Belleville: Mika Publishing, 1972. Reprint of 1898 edition.

Paquette, Lisa, and Jack Ramieri, Jenny Varga, compilers, *How To Trace Your Roots in Essex County: A Source Guide*. Windsor: Windsor Public Library, 1984.

Penrose, Maryly B., *Indian Affairs Papers, American Revolution*. Franklin Park, NJ: Liberty Bell Associates, 1981.

Penrose, Maryly B., *Mohawk Valley in the Revolution: Committee of Safety Papers and Genealogical Compendium*. Franklin Park, NJ: Liberty Bell Associates, 1978.

Poole, Thomas W., *A Sketch of the Early Settlement and Subsequent Progress of the Town of Peterborough and of Each Township in the County of Peterborough*. Peterborough: Peterborough Review, 1967. Reprint of 1867 edition.

Powell, Janet, *Annals of the Forty*. Grimsby: Grimsby Historical Society, 1950-59.

Pringle, Jacob, *Lunenburgh or the Old Eastern District*. Belleville: Mika Publishing, 1980. Reprint of 1890 edition.

Reaman, G. Elmore, *Trail of the Black Walnut*. Toronto: McClelland & Stewart, 1979. Reprint of 1957 edition.

Reaman, G. Elmore, *The Trail of the Huguenots in Europe, the United States, South Africa and Canada*. Toronto: Thomas Allen Ltd., 1963.

Reynolds, Nila, *In Quest of Yesterday*. Minden: County of Haliburton, 1968.

Ringereide, Mabel, *The Flourishing Tree*. Ottawa: Heritage House Publishers, c 1979.

Robertson, John Ross, *Landmarks of Toronto, A Collection of Historical Sketches of the Old Town of York from 1792-1833 and of Toronto from 1834-1914*. Belleville:Mika Publishing [Vols. 1 and 3], 1976 and 1974. Reprints of older editions c 1894-1914.

Scott, James, *The Settlement of Huron County*. Toronto: Ryerson Press, 1966.

Speers, Jan, and Ruth Holt, *Research in Halton and Peel: A Genealogical Handbook*. Oakville: Halton-Peel Branch OGS, 1981. Revised 1984.

Speers, Jan, and Margaret Williams, *People of Halton: Indexes to Genealogical Sources in Halton*. Oakville:Halton-Peel Branch OGS, 1983.

Storey, Anne, *The St. George's Society. A History and List of Members of 1834-1967*. From the author, 820 Burnhamthorpe Rd., Apt. 107, Etobicoke, Ontario M9C 4W9 ($10).

Stuart, Donna V., Editor, *Michigan Censuses 1710-1830*. Detroit: Detroit Society for Genealogical Research, 1982.

Taylor, Ryan, *Family Research in Waterloo and Wellington Counties*. Kitchener: Waterloo-Wellington Branch OGS, 1986.

Turk, Marion G, *The Quiet Adventurers*. Detroit: Harlo Press, 1971.

United Counties of Northumberland and Durham, 1767-1967. Cobourg: Centennial Book Committee, 1967.

Walker, Harry J., *Carleton Saga*. Ottawa: Runge Press, 1968.

Walls, Bryan Earl, *The Road That Led to Somewhere*. Windsor: Olive Publishing, 1983.

Wanamaker, Loral and Mildred, *Abstracts of Surrogate Court Wills, Kingston and Vicinity, 1790-1858*. Kingston: Kingston Branch OGS, 1982.

Warrilow, Betty, *Tracing Your Ancestors in Bruce and Grey*. Bruce and Grey Branch OGS, 1982.

Western Ontario Historical Notes. London: University of Western Ontario, 1942-72.

Yeager, William R., *Searching For Your Ancestors in Norfolk County*. Simcoe: Norfolk Historical Society, 1976.

Yeager, William R., *Wills of the London District 1800-1839*. Simcoe: Norfolk Historical Society, 1979.

York Pioneer, The. Toronto: York Pioneer and Historical Society, 1906-.
York, Upper Canada, Minutes of Town Meetings and Lists of Inhabitants, 1793-1823.
   Toronto: Metropolitan Toronto Library Board, 1984.

Index